Middle School English Teacher's Guide to Active Learning

Marc V. Moeller

Victor J. Moeller

Routledge
Taylor & Francis Group
New York London

First Published 2000 by Eye On Education

Published 2013 by Routledge
711 Third Avenue, New York, NY, 10017, USA
2 Park Square, Milton Park, Abingdon, Oxon OX14 4RN

Routledge is an imprint of the Taylor & Francis Group, an informa business

Library of Congress Cataloging-in-Publication Data

Moeller, Marc V., 1970-
Middle school English teacher's guide to active learning / by Marc V. Moeller and Victor J. Moeller.
p.cm.
Includes bibliographical references.
1. English language—Study and teaching (Secondary) 2. Reading (Secondary) 3. Active learning. I.Moeller, Victor J., 1937- II. Title.

ISBN 1-883001-87-0
ISBN: 978-1-883001-87-2 (pbk)

Also Available from Eye On Education

High School English Teacher's Guide to Active Learning
by Victor J. Moeller and Marc V. Moeller

An English Teacher's Guide to Performance Tasks and Rubrics: High School
by Amy Benjamin

An English Teacher's Guide to Performance Tasks and Rubrics: Middle School
by Amy Benjamin

Writing in the Content Areas
by Amy Benjamin

The Paideia Classroom
by Terry Roberts with Laura Billings

Collaborative Learning in Middle and Secondary Schools
by Dawn M. Snodgrass and Mary M. Bevevino

Teaching English in the Block
by Joseph Stzepek, Jeffry Newton, and Dan Walker, Jr.

Socratic Seminars in the Block
by Wanda H. Ball and Pam Brewer

Personalized Instruction
by James W. Keefe and John M. Jenkins

The Interdisciplinary Curriculum
by Arthur K. Ellis and Carol J, Stuen

Coaching and Mentoring First Year and Student Teachers
by India J. Podsen, and Vicki M. Denmark

TABLE OF CONTENTS

ACKNOWLEDGMENTS

"We are as pygmies standing on the shoulders of giants."

Saint Bernard of Clairvaux

I must give credit where it is due. Much of what I know about the Socratic method of teaching, I learned during my 14 years (1967-81) as an in-service instructor for the Great Books Foundation of Chicago and from my mentor Mortimer Adler. While most of the ideas that I present here are my own, in that I have developed and refined them over the last 35 years in the classroom, the seminal ideas are found in Adler's writings and the training manuals of the Great Books Foundation. No book by itself can make anyone a competent Socratic teacher; only a good training course, sustained practice, and effort over time will make that difference. Therefore, I recommend two:

1. Great Books Foundation, Chicago for their national schedule of training dates near you (www.greatbooks.org).
2. The program of the National Council for Excellence in Critical Thinking (www.criticalthinking.org/ncect.ncik).

MEET THE AUTHORS

Victor J. Moeller has taught Composition, Rhetoric, American Literature, World Literature, Journalism, Creative Writing, and other courses at several different high schools. He was an in-service field instructor and Area Director for the Great Books Foundation for 14 years. During that time he conducted the Great Books Foundation Basic and Advanced Leader Training course in 36 states. He has Master degrees in English and in Education. Victor Moeller currently teaches at Jacobs High School in Algonquin, Illinois, and may be reached by e-mail at moeller@mc.net or at http://user.mc.net/~moeller/

Marc V. Moeller has taught courses at both high schools and middle schools ranging from AP English (Rhetoric and English Literature) to English as a Second Language. He has a Master's degree in Education from National Louis University in Chicago. He states that the greatest influence on his teaching career has been Victor Moeller, his father and mentor. Marc Moeller currently teaches English at Barrington Middle School in Illinois, and may be reached by e-mail at www.marcanna@chicago.avenew.com.

PREFACE

"Learning is not a spectator sport."

- Teachers talk too much.
- Telling a student to think is like telling a pig to fly.
- There can be no learning without discipline.
- The school that fails to teach thinking, fails in everything.
- The student, not the teacher, is the primary agent of learning.
- Nothing is more daunting for a teacher than to get a student to think.
- Teaching is not chiefly about passing out information.
- The best kind of discipline is to engage students in engrossing activities.
- If thinking were easy, there would be more of it.
- The role of the teacher is to uncover the question that the answer hides.
- Thoughtful teachers create thoughtful students.
- Thinking is a skill that has to be practiced daily, like playing a piano.
- Authentic learning begins when teachers confront students with problems about meaning—real questions—that demand solutions.

Dear Colleague,

If you agree with most or at least some of the above statements, you have found a kindred spirit. As I shake your hand and get a chair for you, let me explain briefly how this book will help you become a better teacher. Everything in this text is based on the assumption that students, not teachers, are the primary agents in learning. The corollary is that authentic learning is active learning. The consequence is that students become responsible for their own learning.

I have been writing this book in my imagination for the last 30 years. It describes, illustrates, and explains how to engage your students in a variety of active learning activities. However, just as no book on tennis, for example, can make you a good tennis player so neither can a book, on active learning, by itself, make you a proficient teacher. Nevertheless, with sustained effort, practice, experimentation, guidance, and willingness to learn from your mistakes, and with the use of video film, you can learn how to become an active learner along with your students.

To get a better idea of what I do with my students, check out my English Student Home Page (htttp://user.mc.net/~moeller/). If you have questions, comments, or suggestions, I would love to hear from you because it is, after all, for teachers like you that this book was assembled (moeller@mc.net).

Finally, while I teach high school students, my son Marc teaches in middle school. For most of these active learning strategies, he has provided corresponding, classroom tested and refined materials for grades six through eight.

Victor J. Moeller

1

Two Models of Teaching

If Good Teaching Is a Dialogue, Why Does the Little-Red-Schoolhouse Method Continue to Dominate?[1]

Robert Benchley once remarked that "There are two kinds of people, those who classify things and those who don't." Because I belong to the first group, I tend to classify teachers according to those who still employ the little-red-schoolhouse model of learning (lecture) and those who daily engage their students in active learning. I do so not only because most of my former teachers assumed that they were the most important part of the learning process, but also because the lecture method still dominates among many teachers even today. In contrast, the so-called Socratic teacher knows that the student is the most important part of the learning process.

Take my high school American literature teacher, Mr. Prosser. He began most lessons by stating the objective—"By the end of this class you will be able to identify the characteristics of the *code hero* in Hemingway"—and then, anticipating the so-what looks on our faces, explained the relevance or importance of this knowledge: "Hemingway's concept of the *code hero* will give you standards

1 An edited version of this introductory chapter written by Victor J. Moeller, "Hail, Socrates," appeared in *Teacher*, 62–63 (May-June, 1999).

by which to judge your own ideas about heroism." The class proceeded as a lecture. Mr. Prosser knew what a *code hero* was and he was going to tell us, tell us that he told us, and then ask us to tell him what he had told us. Our job as students was to *pay attention*, that is, to be receptive and passive and to take careful, detailed notes. We were not to interrupt his lecture with comments; however, we were allowed to ask questions for elementary clarification. For example: "What do you mean by pragmatic?" or "Who is James L. Roberts?" or "Why do you call this stuff literary criticism?" His authority was supreme, his answers all we needed to know on those subjects. After all, he had a master's degree.

His lessons concluded with an objective test. "I am the tester, and you are the testees," he would say, and never would we break from those roles. However, "to be fair"—another of his pet phrases—he "entertained" questions before the test. If we had none, Mr. Prosser judged his lesson a success. In the end, we were to trust that Mr. Prosser knew best even when we did not know what he was talking about. "Someday you will understand, and all will be clear," he would reassure us.

I eventually came to understand, thanks to my college contemporary literature professor Kenelm Basil, that there was a better way to teach. Mr. Basil was a Socratic teacher if ever there was one. He began each lesson not by telling us what we were going to learn (he was not certain that we would learn anything although that was, of course, his fondest hope) but by posing a major problem about the meaning of the day's assigned reading. He always began with a basic question of interpretation, wrote it on the board, and then asked each of us to write down our own initial answers on scrap paper. For example, "According to Vonnegut's story, *Harrison Bergeron*, is the desire to excel as strong as the tendency to be mediocre?" Because he kept his own opinions to himself—he was not a participant but a leader—and asked only follow-up questions on our responses, Mr. Basil convinced us over time that he really did not have a single correct answer in mind. Indeed, the class came to realize that more than one correct answer was possible because evidence from the story supported both sides of the issue. In short, our teacher began the discussion with a real question, the answer to which he himself was uncertain.

As students, we had to be active: clarifying our answers, testing others' answers for supporting evidence, resolving conflicting answers with evidence, and listening for more opinions. Learning in Mr. Basil's classroom was not about receiving ideas but about wrestling with them. The test of truth was reason and evidence, not teacher authority. The lesson concluded with a resolution activity since, after all, questions are quests for answers. We were asked to review our original responses and then to write a one-page essay stating our comprehensive answer to the basic question. Mr. Basil strove not for group consensus or truth by vote, but rather for individual understandings: "Given the answers that you have just heard in discussion, what now is your solution?"

Liberation at last! I no longer had to sit dutifully silent while someone told me what I could just as easily have read for myself, found in a library, or researched on the Internet. I no longer had to parrot the teacher's interpretations. More importantly, Mr. Basil challenged me to think independently and to become responsible for my own ideas. The responsibility for learning had been placed in my hands and along with it, the joy and personal satisfaction of arriving at my own insights. I had learned to live with doubt and to uncover questions that answers hide. In short, I had learned how to learn.

Do not misunderstand. Many so-called Socratic teachers do not conduct discussions the way Mr. Basil did. Many have not mastered the art of fostering reflective, independent thinking. Such teachers confuse the right to express an opinion with the notion that any opinion can be right. Toleration of any and all ideas becomes the goal, and brainstorming—that pathetic analogy—gets enthroned as the method. As one mindless person put it, "Don't we all know that everything is relative and that there are no absolutes?" Except, of course, this opinion.

Others, the pseudosocratic teachers, offer little more than a disguised lecture. These teachers pretend to conduct open discussions but have specific answers in mind. They tip their hands in several ways: by asking leading questions, "How can you honestly think Vonnegut would agree with you?"; by allowing opinions that they agree with to go unchallenged or unsubstantiated; by developing a single line of argument or one side of an issue; by injecting their own opinion into the discussion, "I believe that you have all overlooked important information on page six,"; by commenting on student answers, "That's very good, James. I'm so proud of you" or, "Maria, I think you had better reconsider your answer. You are missing something,"; and, finally, by attempting to arrive at group consensus, "I would like to see a show of hands. How many think the desire to excel is as strong as the tendency to be mediocre."

If what I have said about these would-be Socratic teachers is not true, how else are we to explain the following examples of common student and teacher behaviors:

- Teacher: "Whenever I try to have a discussion, my students clam up. Only one or two contribute. They just don't get the point. I *have* to tell them."
- Student: "My answer is correct, isn't it Mrs. Jones?"
- Teacher: "Discussion is a waste of time. I have to cover the curriculum."
- Student: "But Mrs. Jones, what *is* the right answer?"

- Teacher: "My students' test scores have to improve. I don't have time for the luxury of endless discussions. I have 130 students. Get real."
- Student: "Why do you keep asking questions when you know the answers?"
- Teacher: "Students don't know how to ask good questions and anyway, discussions are just too messy."
- Student: "Just let me alone and give me my C. I don't mess up your class."
- Teacher: "My students cannot be trusted to think for themselves. They keep coming up with silly answers."

But isn't that just the point? The lecturing teacher fails to understand that wrong answers are a necessary part of the learning process when real thinking takes place. In contrast, the authentic Socratic teacher recognizes and accepts false turns and *silly* answers as inevitable when students have the freedom to be wrong—*and* right. After all, thinking *is* difficult and students resist it like a plague. Any teacher will recognize immediately the common cop-outs: " I don't know." or "Why did you call on me?" or "I wasn't doing anything" or "Who cares?" or "What difference does it make?"or "Ask somebody else." In the end, if thinking were easy, there would be more of it.

The fundamental difference between Mr. Prosser and Mr. Basil comes down to who is finally responsible for learning. Mr. Prosser's approach implies that the teacher is, while Mr. Basil's suggests that students should be. Can anyone convince students they are responsible for their own learning other than students themselves? And is it not usually through discussion, dialogue, and problem solving—not through lecture—that students come to realize what they *have*, and *have not* learned?

Not long ago, I heard James Howard of the Council for Basic Education state on National Public Radio, "Education is what you have left after you have forgotten everything that you learned in school." I wonder what Mr. Prosser would make of that statement. I know what Mr. Basil would do with it.

The following outline (Figure 1.1) compares and contrasts the two models of teaching discussed in this introduction.

FIGURE 1.1 TWO MODELS OF TEACHING AND LEARNING

Didactic *Passive Learning* *[Master/disciple]*	*Socratic* *Active Learning* *[Engaged inquiry]*
1. Teacher centered: based on the assumption that the teacher is the primary agent in learning.	1. Problem centered: based on the assumption that the student is the primary agent in learning.
2. Teacher's role: to impart the results of experience, personal study, and/or reflection.	2. Teacher's role: to uncover the question that the answer hides. To be a co-learner.
3. Primarily deductive: the usual methods are storytelling, and use of analogy.	3. Primarily inductive: the usual methods are lecture, discussion, dialogue, and problem solving.
4. Test of truth: authority and/or experience.	4. Test of truth: reason and evidence.
5. Learning is the reception of ideas.	5. Learning is a conflict of ideas: a thesis, an antithesis, and a synthesis that results in new knowledge (Hegel).
6. Student's role: to be passive, open, receptive, trusting, and unquestioning.	6. Student's role: to be active, questioning, critical, and discriminating—to learn to trust one's own judgment (independent thinking).
7. Evaluation is factual recall of data—usually in the form of objective tests and right/wrong answers.	7. Evaluation is application of understanding and interpretation of data—commonly in an essay.
8. Ultimate goal: wisdom viewed as the internalization of truths and beliefs.	8. Ultimate goal: wisdom viewed as an informed ignorance—knowing what one does not know—the Socratic paradox.

AFTERWORD

"The school that fails to teach thinking fails in everything."

Richard Mitchell,
Less Than Words Can Say

While the introduction illustrates the importance of the Socratic method for active learning, the didactic model still has a necessary but minor role because teachers sometimes must also provide organized information not accessible in other ways. Figure 1.2 is a comparison-contrast outline of these two generic lesson plans that reveals importance differences.

FIGURE 1.2 LESSON PLAN MODELS

Didactic *[Infusion]*	*Socratic* *[Discovery]*
1. Anticipatory set: motivator, focus.	1. Attention grabber, focus.
2. Objective: what students will be able to do by end of the lesson.	2. Objective: to solve problems. What students learn cannot be stated in advance.
3. Purpose: why lesson is important, useful, and relevant.	3. Purpose: to increase understanding and enjoyment of the group task and to develop the habit of independent and critical thinking.
4. Input: new information or activities.	4. Input: basic questions of interpretation and the co-leader's prepared follow-up questions.
5. Modeling: verbal or physical example of acceptable finished product or process.	5. Modeling: the co-leaders follow the four rules of Socratic discussion.
6. Checking: for understanding to determine if students have the information needed to complete the task.	6. Checking: co-leaders ask follow-up questions for clarification, and substantiation, more opinion consistency, implication, relevance, and resolution.

7. Guided practice: task done independently or in small groups with teacher assistance.	7. Guided practice: Students learn how to rely on their own judgment about which answers are best and to distinguish the false from the true.
8. Closure: summary of what should have been learned. The objective is restated or rephrased.	8. Closure: a written or oral resolution to the problem(s).

I hesitate to comment on the Paideia model of the Socratic method because it is the conception of Mortimer Adler, my mentor and a founder of the Great Books Movement. Nevertheless, because this model has been canonized, I must comment briefly on three key elements not only to point out where it differs from my method but also because solid reasons make my method superior (which I explain at length in the following chapters).

My chief objection to Adler's model is that *it purports to be Socratic when in reality it is didactic.* The teacher (discussion leader) decides what students are to learn. Thus, this model lacks the essential element of Socratic teaching—focusing learning on real questions, that is, questions that have the vital element of doubt (see pages 15–17). By "real" questions I mean those that have doubt for the leader, not merely for the student. A question has doubt when there seems to be no answer at all *or* when several answers seem plausible but none entirely satisfy.

Another objection that I have to the Paideia model is that the leader's role is more passive than active. It is passive in that the teacher never injects his or her own opinion into the discussion and only occasionally asks follow-up questions for clarification, more opinion, and substantiation. It is active in that the teacher sets the goals, determines the outcomes, and corrects factual errors in discussion when needed.

Finally, the Paideia model suggests that three kinds of questions are to be asked in sequence: the teacher begins with a single, general (a) *opening* question that does not initiate reflective thinking because it is not a *specific* problem about meaning. For example: "What is *Antigone* about?" or "What is Hawthorne's purpose in *The Scarlet Letter*?" After a variety of responses, the leader then asks from two to five (b) *core* questions, that is, prepared follow-up questions about specific lines or paragraphs in the text. After sufficient discussion (30 to 60 minutes), the leader then asks a (c) *closing* question of evaluation that attempts to apply the text to students' personal lives. For example: "Have you ever defied a law or rule because you thought that it violated some higher law?" or "How has Reverend Dimmesdale's guilt helped you better understand human nature?"

In sum, the Paideia model is not really a Socratic method of teaching because:

- Its goal relies too much on what the teacher (leader) thinks students should learn and apply from the text;
- Its teacher is too passive during discussion and puts too much faith in the magic of group dynamics; and,
- Its sequencing of the three questions is artificial, unnecessary, and ineffectual because it does not develop in any disciplined way the habit of critical and reflective thinking.

In other words, this model does not allow students to become responsible for their own learning. Once again, the Paideia model of the Socratic method resurrects the false assumption that the teacher is the primary agent in the learning process.

2

TECHNIQUES OF ACTIVE AND CLOSE READING: FICTION AND NONFICTION

"The person who does not spend at least as much time in actively and definitely thinking about what he has read as he has spent in reading, is simply insulting the author."

Arnold Bennett

A first step for participating in the Socratic Seminar is reading the selection. Far too many students read neither actively nor closely, not only because they have not learned how to discriminate among the various purposes of different kinds of reading, but also because they have not been taught how to read actively. Here is a method that I have found effective if employed continually by teacher and student.

The phrase *active and close reading* immediately suggests two ideas. First, some books and stories deserve to be read closely, slowly, or actively—not only because we would miss many of their implied meanings but also because we must learn to recognize meanings other than our own in what we peruse. Second, there are times when how fast we read or how much we read is of no importance. What *is* important is that we learn to *reflect* on what we read and learn how to carry on a conversation with the author. We converse with an author when we question always what he or she says.

The *purpose* of active and close reading is to learn to read interpretively—to pay attention not merely to *what* an author says but to *why* he says it in the *way* that he does. In short, the purpose in reading is not merely to try to recall what happens in a story, for example, but to think about why things happen as they do. With nonfiction, active readers take particular note of an author's choice of words (diction), use of sentence structure (syntax), and his or her organization of ideas.

Some books and stories like those that we will be reading, can be *interpreted in several ways*. No individual—adult or child, teacher or student—ever thinks of *all* of the possible interpretations in a given selection. As a result, no one can tell you what is *the* correct interpretation of a story, poem, or play—not even, believe it or not, the author! However, this does *not* mean that all interpretations are equally good or correct. On the contrary, some interpretations are better than others and some are wrong. How can this be so? The answer is that some interpretations have more evidence to support them, which makes them more plausible. Other interpretations are more comprehensive, that is, they explain more of the text than others do. Still other interpretations are wrong either because there is no evidence to support them or because the evidence offered is contradicted by some other statement of the author. But what about the author, why doesn't he or she have the last word about what he or she *really meant*? Thomas Mann, in the extraordinary afterword of his novel, *The Making of the Magic Mountain,* says:

> I consider it a mistake to think that the author himself is the best judge of his work. He may be that while he is still at work on it and living in it. But once done, it tends to be something he has got rid of, something foreign to him; others, as time goes on, will know more and better about it than he. *They* can often remind him of things in it he has forgotten or indeed never quite knew.

Just as no one can tell you what *the* correct interpretation is nor what your interpretation must be, so also no one can tell you *what details* in your reading are important. Meaning can begin anywhere—even with what someone else might regard as insignificant detail. Whatever furnishes you with clues for arriving at your own interpretation, that is what is important. In short, what is important varies from reader to reader.

In addition, to interpret a work for yourself does *not* require that you first read about the author's life, or about the times in which the author lived, nor review general introductory or background statements. Instead, a reader can begin by noting his responses to a story and then try to convert as many of them as possible into questions. But to engage in this process fruitfully, a reader must learn to respect his own responses—that is, to take seriously his thoughts and feelings about a book.

THE FIRST AND SECOND READINGS

Forming good questions whose answers can yield a great deal of meaning about a story requires at least *two readings*. Roland Barthes, the eminent French literary critic, maintains that "He who reads a story only once is condemned to read the same story his whole life." On the *first reading*, the reader's main interest should be to note his responses in writing, that is, to make notations. Tom Romano, former Ohio high school English teacher, says that "Reading without writing [here, notations] is like cooking without eating." During the *second reading*, readers note new responses and pay special attention to those notations that they can convert into questions.

Unless a reader learns to put his or her responses into writing, by making notations while reading, he or she will have few questions—or, if there are any questions at all, they will be so general that they could be asked of any story. Such generic questions yield little new knowledge and yet without questions, no one can increase his understanding of the material. The first step to learning then is, paradoxically, knowing what you want to know—that is, asking real questions.

As the American philosopher and educator Mortimer Adler explains in his classic essay "How to Mark a Book," a notation is any response to the text that a reader puts into writing. Notations take various forms: underlining what is important, circling key words, drawing lines to make connections between similar parts, comments, personal emotional reactions, reminders, and even nascent questions. As John Ruskin so aptly remarked, "No book is worth anything which is not worth much; nor is it serviceable until it has been read and reread, and loved, and loved again, *and marked*."

SOURCES FOR MAKING NOTATIONS

Experienced readers have found that whenever they mark up a text, they usually refer to one or more of these four *sources* for formulating questions:

1. *Whatever they think is important* (for whatever reason).
2. *Whatever they don't understand*. Not understanding something means more than circling unfamiliar vocabulary (although it includes this). It also means including notations about a character's motivation, for example, or about why the story begins or ends as it does, or what the author means by making a certain statement or including a certain scene, and so on.
3. *Whatever they like or dislike, agree or disagree with*. In other words, active readers are also careful to note their emotional responses. For

Louise Rosenblatt (1978) this step is crucial—what the reader brings to the text.

4. *Whatever they think is related*—one part of the text to another. A chief concern of the second reading is looking for connections or patterns among various parts of the reading. For example: The repetition of the same word or phrase. The reoccurrence of similar actions. Contrasting words or actions. The place of something in the text (organization).

The preceding material is summarized in handout form in Figure 2.1.

As with so many things in life, whatever we get out of an enterprise is proportionate to the effort we put into it. So, too, with reading. Unless we learn how to become thoughtful, active, and close readers, we will continue to miss many of the implications of what we read and, as a result, will lose the pleasure of increasing our understanding of what we are reading.

To illustrate, consider the following notations (Figure 2.2, p. 14) I have made on a well-known poem based on the four sources and the different kinds of notations. Figures 2.3 (p. 15) and 2.4 (p. 16) expand the discussion of these notations. On the second reading, notice which of these responses I was able to convert into discussion questions.

ON READING NONFICTION

But what about nonfiction? Do these active reading techniques for fiction apply equally to nonfiction? Yes and no. The same basic techniques of making notations, writing questions, and so on apply also to nonfiction which is commonly defined as "all forms of prose that purport to be factual" and that use exposition, argumentation, and fictions only to illustrate. However, with factual prose particular attention must be given to identifying the author's thesis (what) and purpose (why); the author's audience (who); the author's style (how) of writing—diction, syntax, vocabulary, and use of examples; the structure and organization of ideas; the relationships among the principal sections of the text; and above all, the author's tone or attitude toward the author's topic must be determined. As the College Board people continually remind us, "to miss the tone is to miss the meaning."

(Text continues on page 16.)

FIGURE 2.1. TECHNIQUES OF ACTIVE AND CLOSE READING

The *purpose* of active and close reading is to learn to read *interpretively*—to pay attention not merely to *what* an author says but to why he says it in the *way* that he does. In other words, the purpose in reading imaginative literature (fiction) is not merely trying to recall what happens in a story but to think about why things happen as they do. With nonfiction, we have to take particular note of an author's choice of words (diction), use of sentence structure (syntax), and organization of ideas.

Active reading requires a minimum of *two readings*. The purpose of the first reading is to note your responses in writing by making notations. During the second reading you note new responses and pay special attention to those notations that can be converted into questions.

Experienced readers have found that whenever they mark up a text, they usually mark one or all of these *four sources* for formulating questions:

1. *Whatever they think is important* (for whatever reason).
2. *Whatever they don't understand.* Not understanding something is more than circling unfamiliar vocabulary (although it includes this). It includes making notations about a character's motivation, for example, or about why the story begins or ends as it does, or about what the author means by a certain statement or about why he or she includes a certain scene, and so on.
3. *Whatever they like or dislike, agree or disagree with.* In other words, active readers are also careful to note their emotional responses.
4. *Whatever they think is related* —one part of the text to another. A chief concern in the second reading is looking for connections or patterns among various parts of the reading. For example: The repetition of the same word or phrase. The reoccurrence of similar actions. Contrasting words or actions. The place of something in the text (organization).

FIGURE 2.2. *THE ROAD NOT TAKEN* BY ROBERT FROST

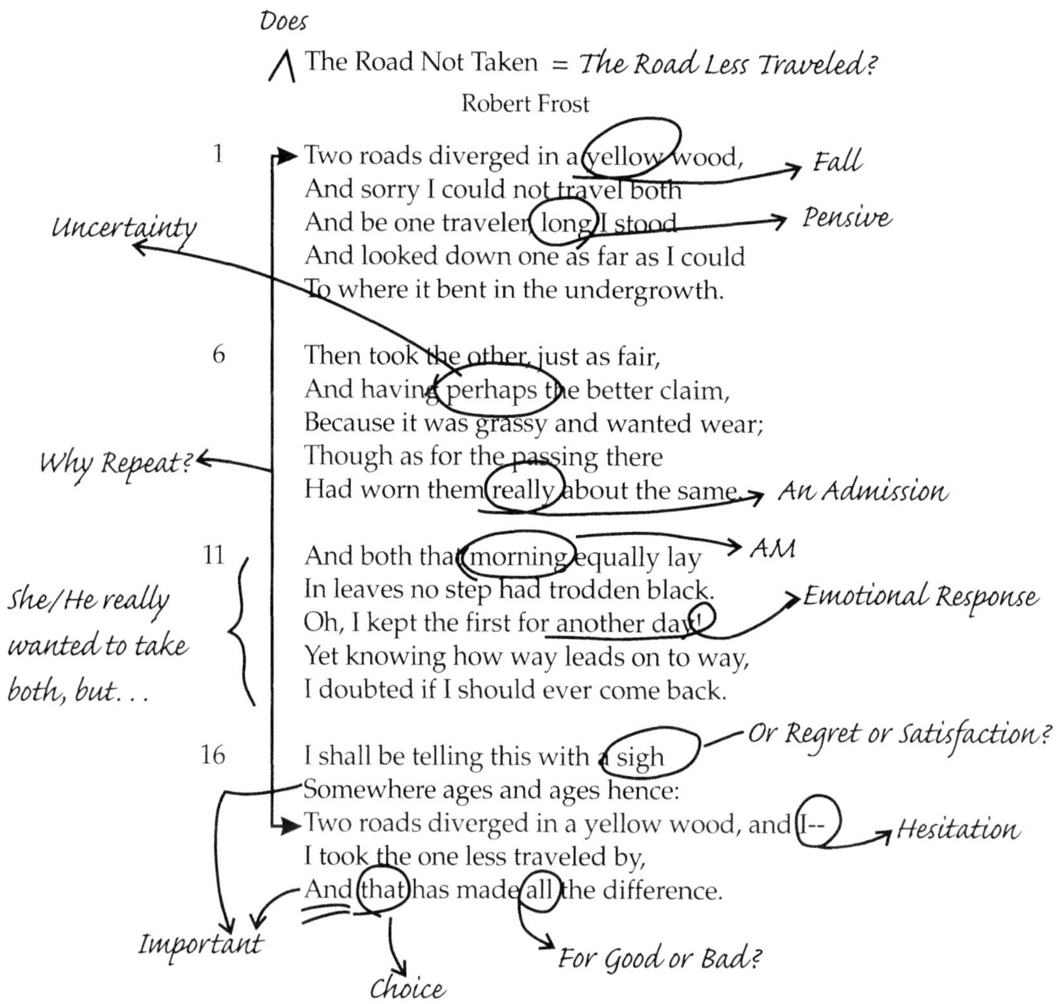

FIGURE 2.3. *THE ROAD NOT TAKEN*: FIRST READING

1. Whatever you think important:

   The speaker really would like to have taken both roads (line 3).

   The speaker admits the two roads were really about the same (10)

   He is talking about a major decision (16)

2. Whatever you don't understand.

   Why isn't the title about the road less traveled?

   Why will the speaker be telling about his decision with a sigh?

3. Whatever you like or dislike, agree or disagree with.

   Whenever I make a choice, I, too, sometimes wonder what would have happenedhad I chosen differently?

4. Whatever you think is related:

   (a) The repetition of the same word or phrase.

   First and eighteenth line.

   (b) The reoccurrence of similar actions.

   Choosing to look back on a previous choice.

   (c) Contrasting words or actions.

   Speaking about a choice and making that choice.

   (d) The place of something in the text (organization).

   Which word(s) of the last line need emphasis?

FIGURE 2.4. *THE ROAD NOT TAKEN*: SECOND READING—NOTATIONS CONVERTED INTO QUESTIONS

1. Why is the title of the poem about the road *not* taken?
2. Why is the choice of the less traveled road made on a fall morning? (1,11)
3. Why would the speaker like to have taken both roads? (2, 13)
4. Why does the speaker say one road had "perhaps" the better claim? (7)
5. Why does the speaker admit both roads were about the same? (10)
6. Why is there an exclamation point at the end of line 13?
7. Is the sigh one of satisfaction or regret? (16)
8. Will the speaker be telling of his choice to others only to himself? (16)
9. Why will the speaker be telling about his decision in future "ages"? (17)
10. Why does line 18 end with a dash?
11. Has the choice of the less traveled road been for the better or the worse?

TEXTUAL ANALYSIS

Textual analysis is a detailed examination of a particular passage in which you try to determine the author's meaning line by line and sometimes word by word.

This technique is a good way to get into a reading when the group has not read well enough to participate in an interpretive discussion. In addition to being a remedial device, when co-leaders use textual analysis, they model what should be happening during the first and second readings. Finally, textual analysis is also effective even when the group is doing well in discussion; in this situation, textual analysis builds on ideas already expressed to draw out more meaning from specific passages that help to resolve the basic question.

Textual analysis involves four steps in this order:

1. *Select a passage* that you want to examine closely and have a group participant read it aloud. Oral reading is not only an important aid

to understanding but also an indicator of a student's level of comprehension of what he or she is reading.

2. *Identify the speaker of the passage,* the narrator. It may be the author speaking directly to you, a fictional narrator, an anonymous narrator, or a character speaking to another character.
3. *Identify the context of the passage.* If you have chosen a passage other than the beginning or the conclusion of the story, try to get a rough idea of where you are in the selection. In short, ask questions about what happened just prior to the passage and what happened just after it.
4. *Review the passage line by line and by key words.* This step is the heart of textual analysis and the most important. Go over the difficult passage line by line, freely asking questions of fact or of interpretation about the meaning of words, phrases, and sentences about which you are uncertain. Freely turn to other sections of the reading that you think are related to the passage being explored. After you have reviewed the entire passage, return to your basic question by restating or rephrasing it and then continue the discussion.

READING ASSIGNMENT

To understand the illustrations used in the following pages of exposition, please read William Saroyan's *Gaston* twice (Figure 2.5, pp. 18–23). On the first reading, make notations on what is important, what you don't understand, what you like or dislike, agree or disagree with, and whatever you find related. On the second reading, convert some of your notations into questions.

Because the first rule of Socratic discussion is that no one may participate who has not done the reading, my students must get 70% on a plot-check quiz of factual questions to join the group. (Nonparticipants must sit in the outer circle of the inner circle of participants.)

When composing a plot-check quiz, avoid questions about trivial details (e.g., Was the father wearing shoes?) and trick questions (e.g., What kind of shoes was the father wearing?). Your purpose is not to punish but to reward those who have done the reading. Figure 2.6 (p. 23) is a sample plot-check quiz.

(Text continues on page 24.)

FIGURE 2.5. *GASTON* BY WILLIAM SAROYAN (REPRINTED WITH PERMISSION)

They were to eat peaches, as planned, after her nap, and now she sat across from the man who would have been a total stranger except that he was in fact her father. They had been together again (although she couldn't quite remember when they had been together before) for almost a hundred years now, or was it only since day before yesterday? Anyhow, they were together again, and he was kind of funny. First, he had the biggest mustache she had ever seen, although to her it was not a mustache at all; it was a lot of red and brown hair under his nose and around the ends of his mouth. Second, he wore a blue-and-white striped jersey instead of a shirt and tie, and no coat. His arms were covered with the same hair, only it was a little lighter and thinner. He wore blue slacks, but no shoes and socks. He was barefoot, and so was she, of course.

He was at home. She was with him in his home in Paris, if you could call it a home. He was very old, especially for a young man—thirty-six, he had told her; and she was six, just up from sleep on a very hot afternoon in August.

That morning on a little walk in the neighborhood, she had seen peaches in a box outside a small store and she had stopped to look at them, so he had bought a kilo.

Now the peaches were on a large plate on the card table at which they sat. There were seven of them, but one of them was flawed. It looked as good as the others, almost the size of a tennis ball, nice red fading to light green, but where the stem had been there was now a break that went straight down into the heart of the seed.

He placed the biggest and best-looking peach on the small plate in front of the girl, and then took the flawed peach and began to remove the skin. When he had half the skin off the peach he ate that side, neither of them talking, both of them just being there, and not being excited or anything—no plans, that is.

The man held the half-eaten peach and looked down into the cavity, into the open seed. The girl looked, too.

While they were looking two feelers poked out from the cavity. They were attached to a kind of brown knob-head, which followed the feelers, and then two large legs took a strong grip on the edge of the cavity and hoisted some of the rest of whatever it was out of the seed, and stopped there a moment, as if to look around.

The man studied the seed dweller, and so, of course, did the girl.

The creature paused only a fraction of a second, and then continued to come out of the seed, to walk down the eaten side of the peach to wherever it was going.

The girl had never seen anything like it—a whole big thing made out of brown color, a knob-head, feelers, and a great many legs. It was very active, too. Almost businesslike, you might say. The man placed the peach back on the plate. The creature moved off the peach onto the surface of the white plate. There it came to a thoughtful stop.

"Who is it?" the girl said.

"Gaston."

"Where does he live?"

"Well, he used to live in this peach seed, but now that the peach has been harvested and sold, and I have eaten half of it, it looks as if he's out of house and home."

"Aren't you going to squish him?"

"No, of course not, why should I"

"He's a bug. He's ugh."

"Not at all. He's Gaston, the grand *boulevardier.*"

"Everybody hollers when a bug comes out of an apple, but you don't holler or anything."

"Of course not. How would we like it if somebody hollered every time we came out of our house."

"Why should they?"

"Precisely. So why should we holler at Gaston?"

"He's not the same as us."

"Well, not exactly, but he's the same as a lot of other occupants of peach seeds. Now, the poor fellow hasn't got a home, and there he is with all that pure design and handsome form, and nowhere to go."

"Handsome?"

"Gaston is just about the handsomest of his kind I've ever seen."

"What's he saying?"

"Well, he's a little confused. Now, inside that house of his he had everything in order. Bed here, porch there, etc."

"Show me."

The man picked up the peach, leaving Gaston entirely alone on the white plate. He removed the peeling and ate the rest of the peach.

"Nobody else I know would do that," the girl said. "They'd throw it away."

"I can't imagine why. It's a perfectly good peach." He opened the seed and placed the two sides not far from Gaston. The girl studied the open halves.

"Is that where he lives?"

"It's where he used to live. Gaston is out in the world and on his own now. You can see for yourself how comfortable he was in there. He had everything."

"Now what has he got?"

"Not very much, I'm afraid."

"What's he going to do?"

"What are we going to do?"

"Well, we're not going to squash him, that's one thing we're not going to do," the girl said.

"What are we going to do, then?"

"Put him back?"

"Oh, that house is finished."

"Well, he can't live in our house, can he?"

"Not happily."

"Can he live in our house at all?"

"Well, he could try, I suppose. Don't you want a peach?"

"Only if it's a peach with somebody in the seed."

"Well, see if you can find a peach that has an opening at the top, because if you can, that'll be a peach in which you're likeliest to find somebody."

The girl examined each of the peaches on the big plate.

"They're all shut," she said.

"Well, eat one, then."

"No. I want the same kind that you ate, with somebody in the seed."

"Well, to tell you the truth, the peach I ate would be considered a bad peach, so of course stores don't like to sell them. I was sold that one by mistake, most likely. And so now Gaston is without a home, and we've got six perfect peaches to eat."

"I don't want a perfect peach. I want one with people."

"Well, I'll go out and see if I can find one."

"Where will I go?"

"You'll go with me, unless you'd rather stay I'll only be five minutes."

"If the phone rings, what shall I say?"

"I don't think it will ring, but if it does, say hello and see who it is."

"If it's my mother, what shall I say?"

"Tell her I've gone to get you a bad peach, and anything else you want to tell her."

"If see wants me to go back, what shall I say?"

"Say yes if you want to go back."

"Do you want me to ?"

"Of course not, but the important thing is what you want, not what I want."

"Why is that the important thing?"

"Because I want you to be where you want to be."

"I want to be here."

"I'll be right back."

He put on socks and shoes, and a jacket, and went out.

She watched Gaston trying to find out what to do next. Gaston wandered around the plate, but everything seemed wrong and he didn't know what to do or where to go.

The telephone rang and her mother said she was sending the chauffeur to pick her up because there was a little party for somebody's daughter who was also six, and then tomorrow they would fly back to New York.

"Let me speak to your father," she said.

"He's gone to get a peach."

"One peach?"

"One with people."

"You haven't been with your father two days and already you sound like him."

"There are peaches with people in them. I know. I saw one of them come out."

"A bug?"

"Not a bug, Gaston."

"Who?"

"Gaston the grand something."

"Somebody else gets a peach with a bug in it, and throws it away, but not him. He makes up a lot of foolishness about it."

"It's not foolishness."

"All right, all right, don't get angry at me about a horrible peach bug of some kind."

"Gaston is right here, just outside his broken house, and I'm not angry at you."

"You'll have a lot of fun at the party."

"Okay."

"Are you glad you saw your father."

"Of course I am."

"Is he funny?"

"Yes."

"Is he crazy?"

"Yes. I mean, no. He doesn't holler when he sees a bug crawling out of a peach seed or anything. He just looks at it carefully. But it is just a bug, isn't it really?"

"That's all it is."

"And we'll have to squash it?"

"That's right. I can't wait to see you, darling. These two days have been like two years to me. Goodbye."

The girl watched Gaston on the plate, and she actually didn't like him. He was all ugh, as he had been in the first place. He didn't have a home any more and he was wandering around on the white plate and he was silly and wrong and ridiculous and useless and all sorts of other things. She cried a little, but only inside, because long ago she had decided she didn't like crying because if you ever started to cry it seemed as if there was so much to cry about you almost couldn't stop, and she didn't like that at all. The open halves of the peach seed were wrong, too. They were ugly or something. They weren't clean.

THE MAN bought a kilo of peaches but found no flawed peaches among them, so he bought another kilo at another store, and this time there were two that were flawed. He hurried back to his flat and let himself in.

His daughter was in her room, in her best dress.

"My mother phoned," she said, " and she's sending the chauffeur for me because there's another birthday party."

"Another?"

"I mean, there's always a lot of them in New York."

"Will the chauffeur bring you back?"

"No. We're flying back to New York tomorrow."

"Oh."

"I liked being in your house."

"I liked having you here."

"Why do you live here?"

"This is my home."

"It's nice, but it's a lot different from our home."

"Yes, I suppose it is."

"It's kind of like Gaston's house."

"Where is Gaston?"

"I squashed him."

"Really? Why?"

"Everybody squashes bugs and worms."

"Oh. Well. I found you a peach."

"I don't want a peach any more."

"Okay."

He got her dressed, and he was packing her stuff when the chauffeur arrived. He went down the three flights of stairs with his daughter and the chauffeur, and in the street he was about to hug the girl when he decided he had better not. They shook hands instead, like strangers.

He watched the huge car drive off, then he went around the corner where he took coffee every morning, feeling a little, he though like Gaston on the white plate.

FIGURE 2.6. MODEL PLOT-CHECK QUIZ FOR *GASTON*

Directions: Answer each question in a brief, complete sentence in the space beneath it.

1. Where do the little girl's parents live?

   The father lives in Paris, the mother in New York.

2. What did the little girl think was unusual about her father's appearance?

   He had a big mustache, wore no shirt, tie, coat, or shoes.

3. How does the girl begin to take on her father's view of Gaston?

   She says they would not squash him and asks if he could live with them?

4. What does the girl want to know about Gaston?

   What would they do with him? Where will he live?

5. How does the mother ridicule the girl's father?

   After she learns about the foolishness that he made up about Gaston, she asks her daughter if her father is crazy.

6. How does the father speak about the girl's mother?

   He does not say anything specific about her mother. If she calls when he is gone to the store, he tells her to tell her anything that she wants to tell her.

7. When does the girl squash Gaston?

   She squashes him after her mother tells her it is okay to do so.

8. Did the father scold his daughter for squashing Gaston?

   No. He asks only why she did so.

9. How did the father say good-bye to his daughter when she returned to her mother?

   He was going to hug her but changed his mind and then shook her hand.

10. How did the father feel as he watched his daughter leave?

    He felt a little like Gaston on the white plate.

With basic and general students, it is sometimes useful to do the first reading in class as a kind of reader's theater. Assign parts, characters, and have students read the story as though it were a radio script. Make the second reading homework. However, review *and* check for notations the next day. Unless you do so, some students will never become active readers because reading with pencil in hand is so foreign and unnatural to them. After all, thinking *is* difficult and until reading becomes a conscious, reflective activity, students will remain mediocre readers. As a result, they will never experience any real pleasure in reading and discovering their own meaning(s).

3

THE SOCRATIC METHOD

"The role of the artist [leader] is to uncover the question that the answer hides."

James Baldwin

OVERVIEW OF THE SOCRATIC METHOD OF DISCUSSION

Let us begin at the source. Like so many students before him and even those today, Socrates' student Meno was exasperated by his teacher's refusal to *just tell him* what to do, what the truth was, and in their dialogue, whether or not virtue can be taught. Meno was astounded when Socrates openly admitted not only that he does not know whether virtue can be taught but also that he does not even know what virtue is. "What!" Meno asks, in Rouse's 1956 translation of *The Great Dialogues*, "Is this the report we are to take home about you?" In characteristic manner, Socrates challenges his student to rephrase the question, to reflect on it, and to arrive at his own answers. In so doing, Socrates helps Meno to wrestle with the implications of the problem that he has posed for their discussion. Indeed, Socrates makes a point of asserting his own ignorance: "All I can say is that I have often looked to see if there are any [teachers of virtue], and in spite of all my efforts, I cannot find them. I do not know what virtue is and, not only that, you may say also, that to the best of my belief, I have never yet met anyone who did know" (Rouse, p. 29). Meno leaves confounded that his teacher, his master and guide, refuses to confirm what Meno believes he already knows.

Nevertheless, when Socrates' reputation for wisdom continues to grow, another impetuous student, Chaerephon, goes to the oracle of Delphi to ask if anyone is wiser than Socrates. The priestess of Apollo, Pythia, replies that no one is. When Socrates hears the answer he is genuinely puzzled: "I have no wisdom, small or great. What can he mean when he says that I am the wisest of men?"

(Rouse 426). But why does Socrates take the oracle's word at face value? Could the god also have meant that no one was wiser than Socrates because wisdom is not to be found among men? Socrates is even more explicit about his ignorance in the defense of his life at his trial, as told in *The Apology.* After questioning another who claimed to be wise, Socrates concludes, "I am better off than he is—for he knows nothing, and thinks that he knows; I neither know nor think that I know. In this latter particular, then, I seem to have the slight advantage over him" (Rouse, p. 327). What we have here is the great paradox of learning: you must first know what you want to know or recognize what you do not know. Is this confusing? Only at first. What Socrates suggests is that the first step to learning is knowing how to ask an honest question—one that you have no answer to or one that you have several answers to but none that satisfy. In short, unless you have questions, you cannot learn. As learning begins, the more you know, the more you realize that you do not know. Such is the Socratic paradox.

But what about the Socratic method? The phrase is as elusive as a greased pig. What does the Socratic method mean to the teacher in the trenches? For some, unfortunately, it means no more than asking a lot of questions—rapidly and indiscriminately. For others, it means conducting an interview. And for still others it means cross-examination. A few even seem to believe that there is something mystical about the Socratic method—that some teachers are born with it or that there really is no common method at all that other teachers can acquire. Nevertheless, all of these notions miss the mark because they fail to capture the Socratic concept of teaching *and* do not recognize that the Socratic method can be explained, applied, and evaluated. Furthermore there is no *official* Socratic method because, even today, there is no consensus about Socrates' method as recorded in the dialogues of his most brilliant student, Plato. Nevertheless, I am bold enough to assert my own conception of *a* Socratic method in the following exposition.

- What is the Socratic method?

  It is an exercise in *reflective thinking* that, according to John Dewey (p. 9) has two elements: *doubt*—a problem about meaning which initiates it—and *an act searching* for (a) solution(s) to solve that problem.

- How is it done?

  It is conducted mainly by asking *prepared questions* (the problems which are the focus of discussion) and *spontaneous follow-up questions* which develop the ideas being considered with a view to achieving resolution.

- Why is it done this way?

  It is done this way to achieve the goal or purpose of this kind of engaged learning: to increase the groups' *and* the co-leaders' understanding (comprehension) of the text under discussion. As a result, there will also be an increase in enjoyment—that is, the satisfaction of discovering one's own answers and finding new meaning(s) in the selection.

Figure 3.1 summarizes this explanation in handout form.

FIGURE 3.1. OVERVIEW OF THE SOCRATIC METHOD OF DISCUSSION

- What is it?

  The Socratic method is an exercise in "reflective thinking," according to John Dewey (*How We Think*). Reflective thinking has two elements: doubt and searching. It begins in *doubt* (a problem about meaning) and then leads to a process of *searching* for solutions to solve the problem (a prepared interpretive question or a basic question). *(Problem)*

- How is it done?

  Socratic discussion is conducted mainly by asking prepared and spontaneous follow-up questions. It begins with a *prepared* question which is the focus or problem to be solved; then *spontaneous* questions move the discussion along and develop the ideas being considered with a view to resolution. *(Process)*

- Why?

  What is the purpose of Socratic discussion? Its purpose is to increase the leader's and the group's understanding (comprehension) of the reading. As a result, there will also be an increase in enjoyment—the satisfaction of discovering one's own answers and finding new meaning(s) in the reading and even one's personal life. *(Product)*

Co-leaders are student pairs, teacher pairs, or teacher-student pairs who have been trained in the *Socratic* method of discussion. But why do you need co-leaders? For several reasons:

- Thinking continuously, keeping track of ideas, and deciding which answers to develop with spontaneous follow-up questions requires a high degree of concentration. Two leaders provide more mental power and ordinarily do a better job than a single leader.
- Two leaders provide a good model of teamwork by working together just as the participants are expected to work together in solving the problem. Co-leaders also instill in the group a belief that they can learn from each other, and a willingness to assume a share of responsibility for the outcome of the discussion. Further, a pair of co-leaders is less likely to be viewed as *authority* figures.
- To follow up ideas and, at the same time, to observe and to recognize those who want to speak, and to invite the reluctant to participate, two sets of eyes and ears are needed.
- Finally, co-leaders need one another to prepare properly for discussion. A co-leader ought never to say to his or her partner, "It is your question, sink or swim with it." On the contrary, it must be *our* previously agreed upon prepared questions that are the focus of discussion and *our* spontaneous follow-up questions that develop and provide the structure needed for authentic learning to happen in discussion.

In summation, the Socratic method begins with a *problem* (a prepared interpretive question), continues as a *process* of asking spontaneous follow-up questions, and results in a *product* (increased understanding and enjoyment).

THE FOUR RULES OF SOCRATIC DISCUSSION

By following these four necessary rules, leaders and participants implement this foundational method of active learning:

1. No one may participate who has not read the selection before discussion.

   The ticket of admission, is that everyone has read the selection carefully. For this reason, before discussion the leader(s) begin with a plot-check quiz, that is, a list of factual questions that anyone can readily answer if he or she has done the reading. Those who have not done the reading are limited to the role of spectators. For less able readers, this rule can be obviated on occasion by making the first reading an oral one in class. Another helpful technique is to conduct textual analysis at times when a group is not well prepared.

2. Participants must support their answers with textual evidence.

   Without evidence, discussion soon becomes a matter of sheer conjecture wherein one idea begins to sounds as good as another. Without evidence participants have no way of deciding which answers are better than others and which are wrong. Evidence turns opinion into interpretation. After all, there are right and wrong answers in discussion just as some answers are better than others are.

3. Participants may not introduce outside authorities but must discuss only the assigned readings.

   This rule ensures that everyone has equal access to the same information upon which everyone has to base his or her answers. The logical starting point for discussion is the reading itself. In their *Theory of Literature*, Warren and Welleck (1956) get to the heart of the matter: "The natural sensible starting point for work in literary scholarship is interpretation and analysis of the works of literature themselves. After all, only the works themselves justify all our interest in the life of an author, in his social environment, and the whole process of literature. But curiously enough, literary history has been so preoccupied with the setting of a work of literature that its attempts at analysis of the works themselves have been slight in comparison with the enormous efforts expended on the study of their background" (p. 127). Furthermore, students learn to become responsible for their own ideas when they do not try to justify them by appealing to an authority—another book or another person. They must learn to rely on their own judgment about the meaning of the text itself.

4. Most importantly, the co-leaders may only ask questions.

   The moment the co-leaders begin making statements during discussion, the atmosphere changes from independent thinking and mutual inquiry to attempts to please the leaders. Even worse, the vociferous can quickly turn discussion into an argument or debate. Furthermore, no matter how well intentioned, leaders' comments hinder the participants' opportunity to think independently and freely. And finally, the co-leader's primary role to develop and relate ideas becomes practically impossible when one or both become participants.

Figure 3.2 presents the four rules of Socratic discussion in handout form.

FIGURE 3.2. FOUR RULES OF SOCRATIC DISCUSSION

1. No one may participate who has not read the selection before discussion.

   The ticket of admission is that everyone has read the selection carefully. For this reason, before discussion the leader(s) begin with a check quiz, that is, a list of factual questions that anyone can readily answer if he or she has done the reading. Those who have not done the reading are limited to the role of spectators. *Note:* For less able readers, conducting an oral reading in class can obviate this rule.

2. Participants must support their answers with textual evidence.

   Without evidence, discussion soon becomes a matter of sheer conjecture wherein one idea begins to sounds as good as another. Without evidence participants have no way of deciding which answers are better than others and which are wrong. Evidence turns opinion into interpretation. This rule also ensures that everyone has equal access to the same information upon which each must base his or her answers.

3. Participants may not introduce outside authorities but may discuss only the assigned reading.

   Students learn to become responsible for their own ideas when they do not try to justify them by appealing to an authority—another book or another person. They must learn to rely on their own judgment about the meaning of the text.

4. Most importantly, the leader(s) may only ask questions.

   The moment the leader(s) begin making statements during discussion the atmosphere changes from independent thinking and mutual inquiry to attempts to please the leader. Even worse, the vociferous can quickly turn discussion into an argument or debate. Furthermore, no matter how well intentioned, leader comments hinder participants' opportunity to think independently and freely. Finally, the leader's primary role to develop and relate ideas becomes practically impossible when he or she also becomes a participant.

THREE KINDS OF QUESTIONS

"What does it say? What does it mean? Is it true?

Mortimer Adler,
A Guide for Leaders of Great Books Discussion Groups (1951)

When did you first realize the importance of the kinds of questions that you ask your students? Was it when you were puzzled about why some questions fell flat while others provoked immediate response? Was it when you suddenly realized your questions were not clear? Was it when you knew that you placed too much emphasis on factual or memory questions? Was it when you got into *bull sessions* as a result of emphasizing evaluative questions? Whatever the moment of insight, few teachers would deny the importance of writing and asking good questions. On the other hand, my experience has been that while teachers recognize that questioning is an art, they also too often are at a loss not only about how to write good discussion questions but also about how to sustain them in discussion.

Mortimer Adler, the eminent American philosopher and education reform leader, first formulated the three kinds of questions in 1948 in *A Guide for Leaders of Great Books Discussion Groups.* He asked: "(1) What does the author say? (2) What does he mean? (3) Is it true; does it have relevance to you here today? *Fact, Interpretation, Evaluation*—these are the three levels of questions" (p. 8). In 1956, Benjamin Bloom edited a *Taxonomy of Educational Objectives: Cognitive Domain,* which classified eight educational objectives that used examples of questions for each kind of thinking: knowledge (memory), comprehension, translation, interpretation, application, analysis, synthesis, and evaluation. Ten years later, Norris Sanders popularized Bloom's taxonomy for social studies teachers with useful illustrations in his *Classroom Questions: What Kinds?*

But do teachers need eight kinds of questions? Not in my experience. Too often have I been in workshops where teachers get into vigorous and pointless arguments about identifying types of questions. Bloom's and Sanders' work has its value for developing standardized tests, but for classroom discussion, their added distinctions are not needed since it becomes evident in discussion that translation, application, analysis and synthesis can be put under the umbrella of interpretation. Knowledge or memory questions are factual and evaluation is about personal values and/or experience. In other words, classroom teachers do well enough, as do most of my colleagues, to recognize the vital difference between *the purpose* of each type of question: to check for recall (factual); To check for understanding (interpretation); or to check for personal relevance and application (evaluation).

Here is how I explain and illustrate the three kinds of questions for my students (Figure 3.3). After reading and reviewing notations on a short story—for example the one that you have just read, William Saroyan's *Gaston*, I check for their understanding of these different types of questions with a bonus practice quiz (Figure 3.4). I want to add that teaching students how to recognize *and write their own* interpretive questions can increase significantly their understanding of the reading *even without discussion*. Figure 3.5 (p. 34) illustrates another useful exercise that will give you further practice in testing your own and the group's understanding of the differences between the three kinds of questions. *Gaston* Lesson Plan 1 (p. 60) in Chapter 5 includes the handouts and answer key for this presentation

FIGURE 3.3. THREE KINDS OF QUESTIONS

1. *Factual*: A factual question has but one correct answer. It asks the reader to recall something that the author said or to read a passage from the text where an answer can be found. Its answer depends more on memory than on thinking.

   Example: *To what does the girl compare her father's home?*

   Note: Sometimes a factual question does require some thinking to answer correctly but it is still factual because only one answer is possible based on a careful reading of the text.

   Example: *Does the girl's mother have a low opinion of the girl's father?*

2. *Interpretation:* An interpretive question has more than one correct answer because a difference of opinion about meaning is possible. It asks the reader to explain *what the author means by what is said*. The answer depends more on thinking than on memory or recall.

   Example: *Is the girl's or the father's situation more like Gaston's?*

3. *Evaluation:* An evaluative question asks one to think about his or her own values or experiences. Such questions sometimes ask a reader to consider how he or she would act in a situation similar to one in which a character in the story finds himself or whether he or she has had a similar experience.

   Example: (common experience) *How would you react if someone said you were crazy?*

   Example: (values) *Do you ridicule people who are different or unusual?*

Note: The *test* for distinguishing between the three types of questions is to begin answering the question itself for a half-minute. If you begin talking about the text, the question is factual or interpretive. If it has but one answer, it is factual; if it can be answered in more than one way, or if you have to explain your answer, it is interpretive. In contrast, if you begin to talk about your own experiences or values, if you go outside the text, it is a question of evaluation.

FIGURE 3.4. THREE KINDS OF QUESTIONS: WILLIAM SAROYAN'S *GASTON*

Directions: First, answer each question briefly. Second, at the left, label the type of question as *Fact* for factual, *Int* for interpretation, and *Eval* for evaluation.

_____ 1. Why does the mother call the insect a bug but the father give it a name and personality?

_____ 2. Did the father buy more than one kilo of peaches for his daughter?

_____ 3. Would you rather live with the little girl's mother or her father?

_____ 4. Unlike the father, why does the mother try to persuade her daughter to stay with her?

_____ 5. Do we know why the girl's parents divorced?

_____ 6. Why does the girl finally decide to live with her mother rather than with her father?

_____ 7. Why does the author have the mother ridicule the girl's father but the father say nothing bad about the girl's mother?

_____ 8. Why do some children of divorced parents have a hard time growing up?

_____ 9. Why does the girl cry before she kills Gaston?

_____ 10. How did the father feel when his daughter returned to New York?

Answer key on page 62.

FIGURE 3.5. WRITING SEQUENCES OF RELATED QUESTIONS: WILLIAM SAROYAN'S *GASTON*

Directions: With your co-leader, write ten interpretive questions on the reading with a page reference for each. Select your two best questions and then write a related question of fact and evaluation for each. Begin with a factual question. For example:

Factual:	How does the father refer to the bug when it appears?
Interpretation:	Unlike the mother, why does the father give the bug a name and a personality?
Evaluation:	Would you have given the peach bug a name?

SIX QUALITIES OF GOOD DISCUSSION QUESTIONS

"What are you asking me, Mr. M—?"

As a teacher, you must have been puzzled at times about why some questions in class fall flat while others evoke immediate response. While student inattention and unwillingness to think may explain some of the lack of response, we must also look at the quality of the questions that we ask. Some questions are so general or unclear that no one could hope for a reasonable response. In short, those questions that evoke next to no response may lack one of the important qualities of good prepared discussion questions, while those that generate ideas for discussion have all the necessary qualities. Here is how I explain and illustrate the six characteristics of good discussion questions (Figure 3.6). Figure 3.7 (p. 36) is an exercise to check how well students understand and can apply the qualities of good discussion questions. *Gaston* Lesson Plan 2 (p. 63) in Chapter 5 includes the handouts for this presentation.

FIGURE 3.6. SIX QUALITIES OF GOOD DISCUSSION QUESTIONS

1. *Clarity*

   A clear question says what it means so that no one has to guess what the questioner has in mind. Using a question that is not clear is like asking someone to find something but not telling him/her what to look for. If the question has to be explained or if it cannot be rephrased, it is not clear. In short, the effort in discussion should be expended on trying to solve the problem, not in trying to figure out the question!

2. *Interpretive*

   Because the primary aim of discussion is to increase your own and the group's understanding of the reading, center on questions of interpretation. In addition, factual questions do not generate discussion since they have but one correct answer. Furthermore, when questions of evaluation become the focus of discussion, too often discussion becomes a bull session.

3. *Specific*

   A good discussion question must be specific, that is, tailor-made so that it could be asked only of one reading and not of another. This is not a matter of being picky or of merely naming a character but is a matter of being precise, that is, of pinpointing a problem.

4. *Doubt*

   There must be doubt in the mind of the person who formulated the question for it to function in discussion. Without the vital element of doubt about the answer to the question, there can be no increase in understanding or insight. A question has the element of doubt *either* when the questioner can think of no answer at all *or*, as is the case more commonly, when the questioner can think of more than one answer but none seem fully satisfactory. In this case, doubt is a matter of degree; it is not complete.

5. *Answerable* on the basis of the text alone

   Avoid questions that go outside the text and ask a reader to offer a speculative answer, that is, one that cannot be supported one way or another from the text itself. Such questions are unsatisfying because with them, one answer sounds as good as another.

6. *Care or concern* about the answer

   Ask questions that interest you *not* what you think might interest someone else. This personal quality adds an intensity to a discussion that is lost without it.

FIGURE 3.7. EXERCISE ON QUALITIES OF GOOD DISCUSSION QUESTIONS: WILLIAM SAROYAN'S *GASTON*

Directions: Which of these questions would be suitable for discussion? At the left of each question, mark *GOOD* if it has the six qualities of good discussion questions. Mark *NC* if the question is *not clear*. Mark *NS* if the question is *not specific* and could be asked of any story with a minor word change. Mark *LD* for *lacks doubt* because it cannot be answered in more than one way. Mark *NI* for *not interpretive* because it is factual or evaluative. Mark *NA* for *not answerable* on basis of the text alone.

_____ 1. What is the main conflict in the story?

_____ 2. Will the girl ever see her father again?

_____ 3. Why does she act like a jerk?

_____ 4. To what does the girl compare her father's home?

_____ 5. Would you have killed the bug?

_____ 6. Does the author portray the girl as confused at times?

_____ 7. Why does the girl describe Gaston's peach as "broken"?

_____ 8. What is the father's role in the story?

_____ 9. Why don't the father and the mother try harder?

_____ 10. Why does the author have the mother try to persuade the daughter to leave but the father refrain from persuading her to stay?

_____ 11. What is Saroyan saying about divorce?

_____ 12. At the end of the story does the father feel like Gaston?

_____ 13. Is the father using Gaston?

_____ 14. Why didn't the father scold his daughter for killing Gaston?

_____ 15. What is the significance of the story's title?

Answer key on page 66.

BASIC INTERPRETIVE QUESTIONS

After you have conducted several discussions, you will observe sooner or later that some interpretive questions require you to look at many lines and passages of a reading and give rise to a number of other related questions about the author's meaning. Those interpretive questions that consistently lead to sustained discussion (about 30 minutes per question) are *basic questions.*

Consider the difference between these two questions on William Saroyan's *Gaston:*

1. Why does the father refrain from hugging his daughter when she returns to her mother in New York? and,
2. Does Saroyan want us to conclude that the daughter or the father has more in common with Gaston's situation?

Both questions are interpretive, but the first is fairly easy to resolve. You could probably find some satisfactory answer just by rereading the conclusion of the story. Because the daughter has made clear that she wanted to return to her mother, the father does not want to put a guilt trip on her—that is, make her feel bad about leaving him. Unlike the mother, the father is careful not to manipulate the feelings of his daughter.

In contrast, to satisfactorily answer the second question, you would likely have to explore a number of related questions. For example: Why does the father say that Gaston could only *try* to live in their house? Why does the father think it unfair for people to holler when someone comes out of their house? Is the father trying to tell his daughter that she, like Gaston, is "out in the world and on [her] own now"? Why does the girl describe Gaston's house as "broken"? Why does the author imply that the girl is as confused as Gaston? Why does the girl say that her father's house is like Gaston's? Why does the story end with the father feeling only "a little" like the squashed Gaston? And so on.

These additional questions, and others you might think of that have something to do with whether the father's or the daughter's situation is more like Gaston's, would obviously take a great deal more time to answer than would the first question about why the father doesn't hug his daughter when she leaves him. In short, the second question is *basic* because it deals with a major issue or problem in the story that requires you to interpret a great deal of the story before you could answer it in a comprehensive and satisfactory way.

Centering discussion on basic questions has two advantages. First, they add a new dimension to thinking about interpretive questions because they require you to organize more facts and ideas to deepen your understanding of the story. Second, basic questions yield a more comprehensive and integrated explanation of the author's meaning than you would have discussing interpretive questions that cover an assortment of unrelated topics or problems about meaning.

But how do you find and write basic questions for discussion? There are two methods:

1. Begin by choosing any interpretive question that you care about and then try to write a number of questions that are related to it and help explore its implications.
2. After you have written at least 20 interpretive questions on the reading, look for a pattern or common topic to which some of them seem to be related.

Whichever method you use, the goal is to formulate a *cluster* of related questions. Hence, a basic question is defined as *a cluster of at least eight related interpretive questions, each of which is a distinct problem for discussion.* In other words, each subquestion or follow-up question is an aspect or a piece of a comprehensive answer to the basic question. Like all interpretive questions these follow-up questions should have the qualities of any good discussion question.

In short, the basic question is the *problem* or the focus of discussion; the cluster is the co-leaders' *plan* to solve it, and the reading selection is the *source* of information needed to resolve it.

Figures 3.8 and 3.9 (p. 40) present two models that illustrate the characteristics of good basic questions just described and explained. From these models and the foregoing discussion, we can identify four characteristics of a good *basic* question:

- All questions in the cluster are interpretive;
- All are related to the problem;
- None are repetitious but each is a distinct problem; and,
- There are at least eight questions in the cluster.

The exercises in Figures 3.10 (p. 41) and 3.11 (p. 42) will help you and your students test your understanding of these concepts. *Gaston* Lesson Plan 3 (p. 69) in Chapter 5 has the answer keys for this exercise.

(Text continues on page 43.)

FIGURE 3.8. A MODEL BASIC QUESTION FOR *THE ROAD NOT TAKEN* BY ROBERT FROST

According to Frost, has the speaker's choice of the less traveled road been for the better or the worse?

If it has been for the better, then:

1. Why is the title of the poem about the road not taken?
2. Why does the speaker wish that he could have taken both roads? (line 2)
3. Why does the speaker say that the road less traveled had "perhaps" the better claim? (line 7)
4. Why is there an exclamation point at the end of line 13?
5. Why does the speaker say that he will be telling us about his choice of the less traveled road with a sigh? (line 16)
6. Does the final line of the poem refer to a good or a bad difference?

If it has been for the worse, then:

7. Does the title of the poem refer to the road less traveled or to the road that most people would have taken?
8. Why does the speaker admit, in retrospect, that both roads were really about the same? (line 10)
9. Why does the speaker say he kept the choice of the first road for another day? (line 13)
10. Why does the speaker say he will be telling about his decision "ages and ages hence"? (line 17)
11. Why is there a dash after "I" in line 18?
12. Is the speaker trying to convince himself that he has made the better choice in taking the road less traveled?

FIGURE 3.9. A MODEL BASIC QUESTION FOR *GASTON* BY WILLIAM SAROYAN

Does Saroyan want us to conclude that the daughter or the father has more in common with Gaston's situation?

If the daughter has more in common with Gaston, then:

1. Why does the father describe Gaston as "the grand *boulevardier*"?
2. Does he fail to explain what a grand boulevardier is because he thinks the term applies only to himself?
3. Unlike the girl, who wants to squash Gaston because he is ugly, why does the father think he is handsome?
4. Is the father trying to tell his daughter that she, like Gaston, is "out in the world and on [her] own now"?
5. Why does the father say that Gaston could only *try* to live in their house?
6. Why does the father think it unfair for people to holler when someone comes out of his house?
7. Why does the girl describe Gaston's house as "broken"?

If the father has more in common with Gaston, then:

8. Why does the girl ask *who* the bug is rather than *what* it is?
9. Why does the author imply that the girl is as confused as Gaston?
10. Why does the girl begin to adopt her father's view of Gaston?
11. Why does the girl cry just before she kills Gaston?
12. Why does the girl say that her father's house is like Gaston's?
13. Near the end of the story, why does Saroyan refer to the father as *the man*?
14. Why does the story end with the father feeling only "a little" like the squashed Gaston?

FIGURE 3.10. EXERCISE 1 ON *GASTON*

Basic Questions:

1. Why does the father let his daughter make up her own mind instead of telling her what to do?
2. Does the author intend the little girl's situation to be like Gaston's?

Directions: For each question below, put a *1* in front of those related to the first basic question and a *2* in front of those that are related to the second.

_____ 1. Why doesn't the father make plans with his daughter about what they would do?

_____ 2. Are we to believe that the girl's home, like Gaston's, can never be in order again because of her parent's divorce?

_____ 3. Why does the father answer with questions when his daughter asks if he is going to squash Gaston or holler?

_____ 4. Why does the father let his daughter decide whether to go with him to buy a peach or to stay at home?

_____ 5. Is the girl homeless in a sense because she is divided in her loyalty to her father and her mother?

_____ 6. Why does everything seem wrong with Gaston just after the mother's phone call?

_____ 7. Is the author suggesting that the girl, like Gaston, cannot live happily in her father's house?

_____ 8. Why doesn't the father tell the girl what to say if her mother calls, except that he has gone to get her a bad peach?

_____ 9. Why doesn't the father comment when his daughter says, "I want to be here"?

_____ 10. Is the "break" in Gaston's house intended to suggest the break in the girl's life when her parents divorced?

_____ 11. Why does the father ask his daughter why she squashed Gaston instead of scolding her?

_____ 12. Why is Gaston wandering around confused after the telephone call?

_____ 13. If the little girl's situation is like Gaston's, why does the author have both her and her father say Gaston is like him?

_____ 14. Why does the father resist his impulse to hug his daughter as she leaves?

_____ 15. Why does the father say only "Oh" when his daughter says she is flying back to New York?

_____ 16. Why does the girl's crying after she squashed Gaston remind her of when she cried "long ago"?

Answer key on page 70.

FIGURE 3.11. EXERCISE 2 ON *GASTON*

Directions: Put an *X* next to any of the questions in the cluster of this basic question, that lack one of the six qualities of a good prepared discussion question. On a separate sheet of paper, revise or replace those questions that are not appropriate.

Why does Saroyan give the girl a mother and father who are so different?

_____ 1. Why does the author have the mother and father live in different countries?

_____ 2. Why does the mother call the insect a bug while the father gives it a name and a personality?

_____ 3. Where does the father live?

_____ 4. Would you rather live with the little girl's mother or father?

_____ 5. Why does the mother try to persuade the girl to leave but the father not try to persuade her to stay?

_____ 6. What is the main conflict in the story?

_____ 7. Will the girl ever see her father again?

_____ 8. Why does the author have the mother send the chauffeur to pick up the girl instead of coming herself?

_____ 9. Do the mother and father both have the best interest of the girl in mind?

_____ 10. Why does the author have the father buy two kilo of peaches before he finds some with flaws in them?

_____ 11. At the end of the story why does the father feel like Gaston?

_____ 12. How long have the girl's parents been divorced?

_____ 13. Why does the author have the mother appear to be richer than the father?

_____ 14. Unlike the father, why is the mother full of plans for her daughter?

_____ 15. Why does only the insect have a name in the story?

_____ 16. To whom does the author compare the girl's father?

Answer key on page 71.

SPONTANEOUS FOLLOW-UP QUESTIONS

"The role of the artist [leader] is to uncover the question that the answer hides."

James Baldwin

Why do some discussions fail even when you know that you began with a good interpretive question? Without doubt, such discussions so often fall flat, go nowhere, become chaotic, or degenerate into *bull sessions* because the leader(s) do not listen to what they hear. As a result, they miss opportunity after opportunity to follow-up on the ideas of the participants. A further consequence is that because answers are not developed, no one has any sense of satisfaction or gain in understanding.

The chief role of the co-leaders in discussion is to direct traffic, that is, to direct and control the flow of ideas among the participants. Co-leaders fulfill this role by introducing *prepared* questions to initiate discussion, basic or otherwise, *and* by asking *spontaneous* follow-up questions to develop and connect ideas that help solve the problem(s) under discussion. By following the four guidelines listed below, you will lead an effective discussion that increases your own and the group's understanding of the reading. As a result, you will also increase your mutual enjoyment of the reading, *the ultimate goal of the Socratic seminar.*

1. If you remember that there is no such thing as a perfect or ideal follow-up question, you will not make your role more difficult by trying to second guess yourself. In other words, there are several distinct kinds of follow-up questions that could be asked at any given moment of discussion. *The kind of follow-up question to be asked in a specific situation depends on the leader's purpose:*

   - Is it to *clarify*? ("What did you mean when you said...?" or "Could you explain more of what you mean by...?")
   - Is it to *substantiate*? ("Upon what in the reading are you basing your answer?" or "How do you know? What in the reading gave you that impression?")
   - Is it to *get more opinion*? ("Maria, do you agree with John's idea that...? If so, could you explain? If not, why do you disagree?")
   - Is it to *test for consistency*? ("Sarah, if what you say is correct, then how do you explain ...?")

- Is it *to relate* a response to the prepared question? ("Brian, how does what you have just said help answer our question about...?")
- Is it to *draw out* the implications of a response? ("Ryan, are you saying...?" "By...do you mean...?") or finally,
- Is it *to resolve* the prepared question? ("John, at this time what is your best answer to our question about...? or, "Laura, how many different answers have you heard so far to our basic question?")

2. Many more ideas are heard in discussion than can ever be pursued or developed. It is unrealistic, pointless, and even impossible to try to keep track of *everything* that is said in discussion. (It simply cannot be done unless you tape your discussions. I can recommend no better way to improve your leadership skills and those of your students than to tape a discussion and critique it later).
3. As a result, co-leaders must make conscious *choices* about what to pursue, to table, or to ignore in any given response or series of responses. In other words, the leaders' responsibility is to make choices that guide or direct the discussion, that is, which keep the responses of the participants relevant to the prepared question(s) presently on the floor.
4. How often must a leader make a choice about what to pursue, to table, or to ignore? Experience shows that the co-leaders must, on average, ask one follow-up question for every two or three responses. Unless the leaders maintain this average by asking enough follow-up questions, discussion soon reverts to a series of random, unrelated, off-the-cuff comments characteristic of mundane conversation.

Following these guidelines leads to two important conclusions:

- Good discussion does *not* result from asking the right or perfect follow-up question at the right time, since there is no such thing. Rather it results from the effectiveness of the overall pattern of the follow-up questions asked.
- The co-leaders' role in discussion is to develop the ideas of the participants and to connect them to the prepared questions under consideration. In this way, resolution is achieved, new insights are discovered, and enjoyment is increased.

Figure 3.12 is a practice exercise on follow-up questions for *Gaston*. It will help you to understand and to illustrate for your students the kinds and purposes of good follow-up questions. Another purpose of the exercise is to help you help your students to think about how they (as co-leaders) would deal with common situations that often come up in discussion. For example, what follow-up question could a leader ask when there is no response at all; when the response ignores the question; when the response has multiple ideas; when the response is wrong; when the participant does not understand the question; when the response is incoherent (not clear); or when the participant tries to dismiss the question because he/she doesn't want to think about it? A copy of the exercise, annotated for discussion, and a handout on the types of spontaneous follow-up questions are included in Chapter 5, *Gaston* Lesson Plan 4 (p. 72).

FIGURE 3.12. EXERCISE ON SPONTANEOUS FOLLOW-UP QUESTIONS FOR *GASTON*

Directions: Each group below consists of a prepared question and a response given during discussion. After each response, write in what you consider to be a good follow-up question. Remember that the general purpose of any follow-up question (which can be factual, interpretive, or even evaluative) is to get the participant *to reflect* on his or her answer and *to develop* it.

1. Leader: Why does the mother try to persuade her daughter to leave but the father tell her only that the important thing is what she wants?

   Sarah: Because the mother is selfish and more involved with her own feelings. She doesn't even realize that it might be better for her daughter to live with her father. But I wonder why the girl wanted a rotten peach.

   Follow-up question: ____________________

2. Leader: Is the author implying that the girl's house, like Gaston's, can never be put in order again because of her parent's divorce?

   Brian: For sure. All the kids that I know whose parents have split are pretty unhappy people.

   Follow-up question: ____________________

3. Leader: Why does the father answer with questions when the girl asks if he is going to squash Gaston?

   Rachael: What questions?

   Follow-up question: ____________________

4. Leader: Near the end of the story, why does Saroyan refer to the father as *the man?*

   John: I don't have a clue. Call on somebody else. Anyway, who cares?

   Follow-up question: ________________________________

5. Leader: Why does the father resist the impulse to hug his daughter when she leaves to return to her mother?

   Laura: He really doesn't love her at all. She was just something he got rid of.

   Follow-up question: ________________________________

6. Leader: Why does the mother ridicule the girl's father but he say nothing bad about the mother?

   Chris: Because that's what the story is all about.

   Follow-up question: ________________________________

7. Leader: Why does no one in the story have a name except for Gaston?

   Participant: Her father wants to be entertaining. He's a fun kinda guy.

   Follow-up question: ________________________________

8. Leader: Why does the girl ask her father why it is important for her to be where she wants to be?

   Linda: I'll bet that question never occurred to her as being important before that moment.

   Marc: She's probably so confused by this time that she really doesn't understand her situation.

   Dave: Maybe she wants to see if her father would react like her mother. She did ask him what she should say if her mother called when he was gone.

   Follow-up question: ________________________________

Answer key on page 74.

WHAT IS A SOCRATIC SEMINAR?

The Socratic Seminar is a series of extended discussions focused on a single topic or theme or on a series of readings that may or may not be related. The seminar is conducted by a teacher, a teacher-team, or co-lead by students who have been trained in the Socratic Method. Its usual length is a full class period of 50 or 90 minutes, 2 or 3 days a week.

PREPARING CO-LEADERS FOR DISCUSSION

Before students begin to co-lead discussions, an entire period should be devoted to reviewing key topics that will prepare them for the task. *Gaston* Lesson Plan 5 (p. 79) can be used for this purpose. Among the items to be covered are these:

- The four rules of Socratic discussion to insure that the co-leaders understand the purpose of each rule—particularly the rule about only asking questions. A handout for this part is included in the text as Figure 3.2.
- The guidelines for co-leading Socratic discussion to ensure that students clearly understand their role and the purpose of discussion. A handout is included with the lesson plan.
- The pre-meeting of co-leaders to prepare, refine and agree upon the questions to be used in the discussion. A handout for this part of the lesson is also included in the plan.
- The use and importance of the seating chart to insure that students are familiar with this necessary tool. A handout on this part is also included with the lesson plan.

Figure 3.13 is a scenario exercise that suggests a format for conducting a Socratic Seminar. It may also be used in conjunction with *Gaston* Lesson Plan 4 (p. 72), which deals with spontaneous follow-up questions.

FIGURE 3.13. SOCRATIC SEMINAR SCENARIO EXERCISE

Co-leaders: (1) ____________________ (2) ____________________
Group members: (1) ____________________ (2) ____________________
(3) ____________________ (4) ____________________

1. Co-leaders' prepared question: ____________________
____

2. Your answer: ____________________
____

Write down answers offered by other group members:
A1 __________: ____________________
(name)
____

A2 __________: ____________________
(name)
____

Write down your follow-up question: ____________________
____

Write down the follow-up question chosen by the leader: ____________________
____

3. Write down your answer: ____________________
____

Write down answers offered by other group members:
A1 __________: ____________________
(name)
____

A2 __________: ____________________
(name)
____

Write down your follow-up question: ____________________
____

4. Write down your answer: ____________________
____

Write down answers offered by other group members:
A1 __________: ____________________
(name)

A2 __________: ______________________________
(name)

Write down your follow-up question: ______________________

Write down the follow-up question chosen by the leader: __________

5. Write down your answer: ______________________________

Write down answers offered by other group members:

A1 __________: ______________________________
(name)

A2 __________: ______________________________
(name)

Write down your follow-up question: ______________________

6. Write down your answer: ______________________________

Write down answers offered by other group members:

A1__________: ______________________________
(name)

A2__________: ______________________________
(name)

Write down your follow-up question: ______________________

Conclusion: After recording six sequences, review with your class the leader's choice of follow-up questions: What kind of follow-up was asked? What was its purpose? Was it related to the participant's answer? Did it keep the prepared (focus) question in sight?

Finally, before they begin, students must understand that discussion will be evaluated in three different ways: through the teacher's completion of the Criteria for Critique of Discussion form (p. 82) (included with the lesson plan) during the meeting; through a written resolution of the basic question(s) at the end of the discussion; and through a formal follow-up essay on one of the basic questions, which essay will be due a few days later.

CRITERIA FOR CHOOSING READINGS FOR SOCRATIC DISCUSSION

Vital to the success of the seminar is a careful selection of the readings that are, in the end, the real teachers. According to George Anastaplo in *Chicago Public Schools Socratic Seminar,* "The ultimate leaders of the best seminar discussions are the authors of the best books. It is only in the best books that one is likely to encounter the finest examples of minds at work" (p. 12). Indeed, unless the readings are carefully chosen according to the tested and established criteria of the Great Books Foundation (Chicago, IL), there can be no hope of having successful meetings in which a mutual increase in understanding and enjoyment takes place. The following sections explain, in order of importance, the four key criteria for choosing good selections.

THE READINGS MUST BE ABLE TO SUPPORT EXTENSIVE READING AND DISCUSSION

The selections must yield multiple interpretations, that is, they must raise interpretive questions about an author's meaning that is not explicit. Only well-written works that are thematically complex and cohesive can suggest real answers, that is, differing interpretations that can be supported with evidence from the text rather than merely being a matter of personal opinion. While every work of literature requires some degree of interpretation, not all works hold up under an extended analysis. This means that not all so-called *classics* qualify for a Socratic seminar. In other words, if the meaning and intention of a book is transparent to the reader, it cannot sustain a genuine search for meaning because it cannot generate questions that have the vital element of doubt about their answers. For example, as appealing and uplifting as are novels such as Wilson's *Where the Red Fern Grows* and Collier's *My Brother Sam is Dead,* they cannot function in Socratic discussion because they are too thin, their meaning obvious, and their intention transparent.

THE READINGS MUST EVOKE REAL QUESTIONS FOR ADULTS AS WELL AS FOR PARTICIPANTS

This second criterion is but the other side of the coin. Since leaders do not rely on a teacher's manual or refer to an answer key in preparing for Socratic discussion, they must be able to write questions on a selection that are *real, for them, that is,* that yield more than one legitimate answer (at least two) or that *seem* to have no answer at all (complete doubt). In other words, leaders *do not* write questions that they believe someone else may have doubt about. They write questions that *they* have doubt about. Because the leaders' own questions reflect their personal curiosity about the meaning of a work, and because leaders never give their own personal opinions, participants begin to see their teacher(s) and peers in a new role—as active and involved partners in discussion, as co-learners, and not as answer givers.

THE READINGS MUST BE REASONABLY SELF-CONTAINED

The kind of reading that best illustrates this third criterion is the short story. In stories like Saroyan's *Gaston,* or Wilbur's *A Game of Catch,* or Faulkner's *Two Soldiers,* the reader is given all the information needed to arrive at a good grasp of their overall meaning or theme(s). In other words, shorter works are more manageable in discussion and more suited to two readings and to intensive analysis. In contrast, works that are not self-contained, invite numerous questions that cannot be answered on the basis of the text alone. They invite mere speculation, where one answer begins to sound as plausible as another. Longer works, full-length novels, present a real problem with this criterion but this obstacle can be overcome if the reading is carefully divided into chapters that are more or less self-contained. Sometimes, the author makes this division for us. For example, Camus divides *The Stranger* into two clearly self-contained parts and Twain's *The Adventures of Huckleberry Finn* follows an episodic plot that is easily divided for several discussions.

THE READINGS MUST BE AGE AND GRADE APPROPRIATE

As Louise Rosenblatt reminds us in her seminal *Literature as Exploration,* reading is an active process, that is, a *transaction* between reader and story that involves not merely *decoding* the text but, more importantly, recognizing what the student brings to the text—his or her intellectual grasp, emotional maturity, and life experience. Recognition of these three key elements explains why students' interpretations vary, why they ignore or overlook certain elements of the story, and why some interpretations are better (more comprehensive and defensible than others).

Given this fourth criteria, consider these examples: *Flowers for Algernon* would not be an appropriate reading for middle school, but *Running Loose* or *The Giver* is. Similarly, *Sons and Lovers* of D.H. Lawrence would not be appropriate for high school, but *Much Ado About Nothing* would be. Hemingway's *The Killers* (which has a fourth grade readability level) would not be appropriate for middle school, but Richard Wilbur's *A Game of Catch*, Shirley Jackson's *Charles*, or Carson McCuller's, *Sucker*, would be well received. *Lady Chatterly's Lover* ought not be in a high school curriculum, but Ibsen's *A Doll's House* always evokes strong reactions. *Antigone* is beyond the grasp of middle school students but not a western such as *Shane*. *Anna Karenina* is too sophisticated for high school students, but not Jane Austen's *Pride and Prejudice*. In short, teachers' must remember that "in the selection of literary materials to be presented to students, it is *not* enough merely to think of what they *ought* to read.

Choices must also "reflect a sense of the possible links between the readings and the present level of a student's emotional maturity" (Rosenblatt, 1976, p. 42). The implication, then, is that "if the language, the setting, and the theme all are too alien, even a 'great work' [a classic] will fail. Books must be chosen that hold out some link with the student's past and present preoccupations, anxieties, and ambitions" (p. 72).

GUIDELINES FOR WRITING ABOUT AND DISCUSSING MOVIES BASED ON NOVELS OR SHORT STORIES

FOUR PRE-WRITING EXERCISES

- Exercise 1: Make notations on what has been *added, omitted, and retained* from the original story.
- Exercise 2: Make notations on *what is important, what you do not understand,* what you particularly *liked* (something that moved you emotionally) and/or *disliked,* and on *what is related* (one part of the story to another, notice connections).
- Exercise 3: List *10 important differences* between the movie and the short story or the novel.
- Exercise 4: List *10 important similarities* between the movie and the short story or the novel.

GUIDELINES FOR EXERCISES 3 AND 4

You have the option of doing these two exercises with a partner. Put both names on the paper; you will receive the same grade. Unless you follow these guidelines exactly, your paper will be returned (INC) and ungraded.

1. Each difference or similarity between the movie and the text (short story or novel) must be written as *a complete sentence.*
2. In each sentence, *refer to both the movie and the story.*
3. *No two sentences may begin the same way;* the sentence openings must be varied.
4. *Number* each difference or similarity and *skip a line* between each sentence.
5. *Circle* the numbers of what you regard as the *three most important* differences or similarities. Rank in order of importance.
6. As always, use ink (no pencil, ever), write on standard paper (no spiral, ever), and put the proper heading on the upper right-hand corner.
7. Avoid wordiness; try to be as concise as possible. Use active voice whenever possible.

CLUE WORDS FOR DIFFERENCES

but, however, unlike, in contrast, although, as if, on the other hand, still, nevertheless, yet, rather than, despite, in spite of, instead of, contrary to

CLUE WORDS FOR SIMILARITIES

similarly, in like manner, just as, in the same way, like, as, equally, similar to

CLUE WORDS FOR RANKING

first, second, finally, more importantly, most importantly, another, furthermore, moreover, in addition, again, of primary importance, the least, the greatest

MODELS

Two Soldiers by William Faulkner

1. In contrast to the short story, the movie omits the narrator's visit to the colonel's home.
2. Similar to Faulkner's *Two Soldiers,* the narrator is determined to get to Memphis to register for the army with his brother Pete.
3. Most importantly, unlike the short story, which ends with Pete's brother in tears, the movie concludes with the narrator slipping in the door as he says he had to cut a lot of wood.

4

THE THEORY BEHIND ACTIVE LEARNING

Why is there such emphasis today on *engaged learning*, on *authentic learning*, and on *active learning*? The revival and use of the Socratic method and seminar is symptomatic of the rediscovery of James Howard's insight: "Education is what you have left after you have forgotten everything that you learned in school" (Council for Basic Education).

Nevertheless, there is some question about whether these adjectives are but today's new buzz words for teaching and learning or are they old ideas that have been put into *new and improved packaging*? Today, parents, students, administrators, and teachers have become increasingly aware of the importance of active learning because passive learning too often results in no learning at all. Mel Silberman (*Active Learning: 101 Strategies*, 1996) and John Holt (*How Children Learn*, 1967) make clear the fundamental differences between *passive* teaching and learning (didactic, infusion, lecture, or direct teaching) and *active* teaching and learning (inductive, discovery, or problem-centered):

- *Passive learning* reveals several limitations:
  - Student attention decreases with each passing minute;
  - It appeals only to auditory learners and emphasizes memory;
  - It tends to promote lower-level learning (factual content); and
  - It assumes that all students need the same information at the same time.
- *Active learning*, in contrast, challenges students to:
  - Learn how to state information in their own words;
  - Illustrate ideas with their own examples;

- See connections between previous and present knowledge;
- Learn how to ask real questions (that have the element of doubt); and
- Seek information to solve problems about meaning.

The following seminal quotations clearly demonstrate that the controversy between active and passive learning is as old as the contrast between didactic (master-disciple) teaching and Socratic questioning (discovery learning). Are these two methods inherently irreconcilable, as some argue, or are they somehow complementary? Consider how these authors answer the question.

- Alfred North Whitehead, *The Aims of Education* (1929, p. 38):

  In training a child to activity of thought, above all things we must beware of "inert ideas"—that is, ideas that are merely received into the mind without being utilized, or tested, or thrown into fresh combinations....Education with inert ideas is not only useless: it is above all things, harmful.

- Jacques Barzun, *Teacher in America,* "On Thinking" (1944, p. 72):

  It is true that like all gifts of nature, the ability to think cannot be imparted; it can only be developed, and one of the oldest complaints against schools is that they turn the natural thinker into a learned dunce....Determined thinkers are few. For most people, thinking is dreary uphill work; their mind is set in motion by only a rare stimulus....Thinking is rare; that is one reason it is precious....Thinking means shuffling, relating, selecting the contents of one's mind so as to assimilate novelty, digest it, and create order. It is doing to a fact or an idea what we do to a beefsteak when we distribute its parts through our body....Discussion must not go off in all directions like a leaky hose. It must have a pattern, beginning at a given point and logically reaching another, from which to start again the next day.... There must also be an atmosphere of freedom in which ideas are freely expressed and freely examined, sifted, rejected, and developed....Good discussion calls for the best teachers in their prime and I am convinced furthermore that it accomplishes more than any other form of teaching.

- Gilbert Highet, *The Art of Teaching* (1950, p. 151):

  The tutorial method of teaching was invented by Socrates....He was the first who thought that teaching might mean, not pouring new ideas into an entirely empty brain, but drawing out universal truths from the mind in which they already lay concealed....For Socrates, teaching was not merely asking a series of questions, with the aim of exposing the pupil's ignorance or piercing his pretentions. These are negative ends. He had a positive end in view, although that end was concealed from the pupil. He wanted to make every pupil realize that truth was in the pupil's own power to find, if he searched long enough and hard enough, refusing all "authoritative statements" and judged every solution by reason alone....This system is the most difficult, the least common, and yet the most thorough way to teach—it is the right combination of critical method and positive purpose.

- John Holt, *How Children Fail,* "Answer Grabbers or Problem Solvers?" (1964, p. 310):

  We encourage children to act stupidly by boring them, by filling up their days with dull repetitive tasks that make little or no claim to their attention or demands on their intelligence....As a result, most children in school are answer-centered rather than problem-centered....They see a problem as a kind of announcement that, far off in some mysterious Answer land, there is an answer, which they are supposed to go out and find....When we give children answers, we call this "helping them."

- Northrup Frey, *The Educated Imagination* (1970, p. 39):

  Thinking is an acquired habit founded on practice, like playing the piano. How well we do it depends on how much of it we have done, and it is never autonomous. We do not start to think about a subject: we enter into a body of thought and try to add to it. It is only out of long discipline in continuous and structured thinking, whether in a school, in a profession, or in the experience of life, that any genuine wisdom can emerge.

- Eleanor Kutz and Hephzibah Roskelly, *An Unquiet Pedagogy,* "The Student as Active Learner" (1991, p. 365):

  Coming to know is an active process, in which the learner must be engaged in acts of discovery and inquiry; this process always takes place in interaction with others, but most classrooms isolate learners from that kind of interaction. The group in the classroom mirrors the way most people learn outside the classroom....While teachers can establish activities that actively engage students as individuals in their learning....We argue that knowledge, because it is fundamentally shared and social, is fully created and negotiated only in collaborative contexts. So, while helping students become active learners and assume authority for their own learning, teachers must also create opportunities for them to share in knowing and coming to know.

- Mel Silberman, *Active Learning: 101 Strategies to Teach Any Subject* (1996, p. 10):

  When learning is PASSIVE, the learner comes to the encounter without curiosity, without questions, and without interest in the outcome (except, perhaps, in the grade he or she will receive.) When learning is ACTIVE, the learner is seeking something. He or she wants an answer to a question, needs information to solve a problem, or is searching for a way to do a job.

- Theodore R. Sizer, *Horace's Hope: What Works for The American High School* (1996, p. 189):

  Good schools promote the habit of respectful skepticism—respectful in the sense that it rests on evidence and carefully established argument but is ever asking questions such as "Just why might this be so?" and "Is there another way of explaining this situation?" All humans revel in this process of inquiry to some extent. Asking questions captures our minds more readily than memorizing somebody else's answers to yet somebody else's questions. Good schools surely push forward the best of what disciplined minds in the past have sent down to us, but always by displaying yesterday's conclusions fundamentally as questions that always need fresh answers.

- Mortimer J. Adler, *Reforming Education: The Opening to the American Mind* (1977, p. 290):

  The ideal Socratic seminar occurs when the teacher is able to resort only to interrogative speech—when there is no declarative, but only interrogative teacher-talk, only the asking of questions.... The more the seminar is an experience of active learning for the students, the sooner they will become active learners in their reading of texts for future seminars and the sooner they will be able to engage in learning by themselves without the help of teachers, which is the ultimate desideratum of all teaching.

What are we to conclude from these confident assertions of these philosophers of education? Clearly they all, in their own way, argue for an emphasis on active learning over passive learning. And is it not revealing how often they refer, directly or indirectly, to a Socratic method of teaching and learning?

5

PREPARING A SOCRATIC SEMINAR ON *GASTON*

Five lesson plans in this chapter show you how to prepare a Socratic Seminar on William Saroyan's short story *Gaston.* These lesson plans will enable you to apply the suggestions made in the previous chapters.

GASTON LESSON PLAN 1: THREE KINDS OF QUESTIONS

1. Focus:	What questions do you have about this object in my hand? List briefly on overhead or blackboard.
2. Objective:	To understand by identifying the three types of questions that can be asked about a reading.
3. Purpose:	Why are the three types of questions important? To be able to write your own questions. To increase your understanding (comprehension) of the reading by writing interpretive questions. To realize the purpose of each kind of question.
4. Input & modeling:	Review handout on the three kinds of questions. (Below) Complete with examples on overhead. Have students copy examples onto their handouts.
5. Checking:	Review definitions of the three types of questions. Review directions for practice exercise.
6. Guided practice:	Review quiz with entire class. (Answer key p. 62) Peer grading. Bonus points.
7. Closure:	Return to questions that students asked about the object in your hand at beginning of class. Point out which questions had but one answer (fact), could be answered in more than one way based on the evidence (interpretation), and those that were about experience or values (evaluation).

This lesson is set up for a 50-minute period. If you have a 90-minute period in a block schedule, you could extend the guided practice by conducting a discussion on a follow-up reading such as Kahil Gibran's *The Children* or by having pairs write sequences of related questions (see examples on handout). Another option is to have groups of four write 10 interpretive questions on the next reading.

THREE KINDS OF QUESTIONS

1. *Factual*: A factual question has but one correct answer. It asks the reader to recall something that the author said or to read a passage from the text where an answer can be found. Its answer depends more on memory than on thinking.

   For example:

   Note: Sometimes a factual question does require some thinking to answer correctly but it is still factual because only one answer is possible based on a careful reading of the text.

   For example:

2. *Interpretation*: An interpretive question has more than one correct answer because a difference of opinion about meaning is possible. It asks the reader to explain *what the author means by what is said*. The answer depends more on thinking than on memory or recall.

   For example:

3. *Evaluation*: An evaluative question asks one to think about his or her own values *or* experiences. Such questions sometimes ask a reader to consider how he or she would act in a situation similar to one a character in the story finds himself or if he or she has had a similar experience.

   For example (common experience):

   For example (values):

The *test* for distinguishing between the three types of questions is to begin answering the question itself for a half minute. If you begin talking about the text, the question is either factual *or* interpretive. If it has but one answer, it is factual. If it can be answered in more than one way, or if you have to explain your answer, it is interpretive. In contrast, if you begin to talk about your own experiences or values, or if you go outside the text, it is a question of evaluation.

ANSWER KEY FOR EXERCISE ON THREE KINDS OF QUESTIONS ABOUT *GASTON*

Directions: First, answer each question briefly. Second, at the left, identify the type of each question as *Fact* for factual, *Int* for interpretation, and *Eval* for evaluation.

INT 1. Why does the mother call the insect a bug but the father give it a name and personality?

INT 2. Why did the father buy more than one kilo of peaches for his daughter?

EVAL 3. Would you rather live with the little girl's mother or her father?

INT 4. Unlike the father, why does the mother try to persuade her daughter to stay with her?

FACT 5. Do we know why the girl's parents divorced?

No explanation is given.

INT 6. Why does the girl finally decide to live with her mother rather than with her father?

FACT 7. How does the mother ridicule the girl's father?

She asks if he is crazy and says he speaks nonsense.

EVAL 8. Why do some children of divorced parents have a hard time growing up?

INT 9. Why does the girl cry before she kills Gaston?

FACT 10. How did the father feel when his daughter returned to New York?

He felt "a little, he thought, like Gaston on the white plate."

GASTON LESSON PLAN 2: QUALITIES OF GOOD DISCUSSION QUESTIONS

1. Focus:	What kind of question generates a lively discussion? Those that are: clear, specific, answerable on basis of the reading alone, arguable, etc.
2. Objective (what):	To identify and illustrate the six qualities of good discussion questions.
3. Purpose (why):	To write your own questions for discussion that will increase your understanding and enjoyment of the story. To carry on a conversation with the author while reading.
4. Input & modeling:	Review first the checklist on the qualities of good discussion questions (p. 64).
5. Checking:	Review directions for practice exercise (Below).
6. Guided practice:	Review quiz with entire class. Peer grading. Bonus points.
7. Closure:	What kind of question generates a lively discussion? Review briefly the six qualities of good questions.

This lesson plan is set up for a 50-minute period. If you have a 90-minute period in a block schedule, you could extend the guided practice by having students apply the checklist to the ten questions that they wrote for the first reading. Another option would be to explain and illustrate the three levels of doubt in good questions. (Handout below)

A CHECKLIST OF SIX QUALITIES OF GOOD DISCUSSION QUESTIONS

1. *Clarity:* A clear question says what it means so that no one has to guess what the questioner has in mind. Asking a question that is not clear is like asking someone to find something but not telling him/her what to look for. If the question has to be explained or if it cannot be rephrased, it is not clear. The effort in discussion should be expended on trying to solve the problem, not on trying to figure out the question!
2. *Interpretive:* Because the primary aim of shared inquiry is to increase your own and the group's understanding of the reading, center on questions of interpretation. In addition, factual questions do not generate discussion since they have but one correct answer. Furthermore, when questions of evaluation become the focus of discussion, too often discussion becomes a *bull session.*
3. *Specific:* A good discussion question must be specific, that is, tailor made so that it could be asked only of one reading and not of another. This is not a matter of being picky or merely of naming a character but a matter of being precise, that is, of pin-pointing a problem.
4. *Doubt:* There must be doubt in the mind of the person who formulated the question for it to function in discussion. Without the vital element of doubt about the answer to the question, there can be no increase in understanding or insight A question has the element of doubt *either* when the questioner can think of no answer at all *or,* as is the case more commonly, when the questioner can think of more than one answer but none seems fully satisfactory. In this case doubt is a matter of degree; it is not complete.
5. *Answerable* on the basis of the text alone. Avoid questions that go outside the text and ask a reader to offer a speculative answer, that is, one that cannot be supported one way or another from the text itself. Such questions are unsatisfying because with them, one answer sounds as good as another.
6. *Care* or *Concern* about the answer. Ask questions that interest you *not* what you think might interest someone else. This personal quality adds an intensity to a discussion that is lost without it.

THREE LEVELS OF DOUBT IN GOOD DISCUSSION QUESTIONS

To avoid writing and asking questions that lack real doubt in the minds of the co-leaders, they must *begin at their deepest level of perception* or understanding of the text. To do so, they must some-times write a question based on an assumption or a hypothesis. In short, not all questions should be neutral or void of any previous understandings or interpretations.

1. *Neutral:* question the significance of a fact, detail, event, choice of vocabulary, sentence, or phrase. [What is the meaning of X?]

   Examples:

   > Why is the title of the poem about the road not taken?
   >
   > Why does Saroyan have the mother call her daughter while her father is out looking for more peaches?

2. *Assumption:* the question is based on a prior interpretation; this question is not neutral but begins with a prior interpretation. [Because X seems to be true, how do we explain Y?]

   Examples:

   > Why is the poem's speaker so pleased with his choice of the less traveled road?
   >
   > Unlike the mother, why is the father more respectful of his daughter's independence?

3. *Hypothesis*: this question is a guess at meaning or an attempt to explain something in light of something else. The element of doubt here is in *may be*—what may be true. [Does X explain Y?]

   Examples:

   > Has the choice of the less traveled road been for the better or the worse?
   >
   > Does the father refrain from hugging his daughter as she leaves because he does not want to make her feel guilty?

ANSWER KEY FOR EXERCISE ON QUALITIES OF GOOD QUESTIONS FOR *GASTON*

Directions: Which of these questions would be suitable for discussion? At the left of each question, mark *GOOD* if it has the six qualities of good discussion questions. Mark *NC* if the question is *not clear.* Mark *NS* if the question is *not specific* and could be asked of any story with a minor word change. Mark *LD* for *lacks doubt* because it cannot be answered in more than one way. Mark *NI* for *not interpretive* because it is factual or evaluative. Mark *NA* for *not answerable* on basis of the text alone.

NS 1. What is the main conflict in the story? (Could be asked of any story.)

NA 2. Will the girl ever see her father again? (There is no way of knowing.)

NC 3. Why does she act like a jerk? (Who is she? How is jerk to be defined?)

NI 4. To what does the girl compare her father's home? (She compares it to Gaston's open peach.)

EVAL 5. Would you have killed the bug?

NI 6. Does the author portray the girl as confused at times? (Yes, several times)

GOOD 7. Why does the girl describe Gaston's peach as "broken"?

NS 8. What is the father's role in the story? (Could be asked of any character in any story.)

NC 9. Why don't the father and the mother try harder? (Try harder at what?)

GOOD 10. Why does the author have the mother try to persuade the daughter to leave but the father refrain from persuading her to stay?

NS 11. What is Saroyan saying about divorce? (Not enough of a problem)

NI 12. At the end of the story does the father feel like Gaston? (Yes, he says he felt a little like Gaston. But why only a little?)

NC 13. Is the father using Gaston? (What do you mean by using?)

GOOD 14. Why didn't the father scold his daughter for killing Gaston?

NS 15. What is the significance of the story's title? (Could be asked of any story. Why do you want to know about the title?)

QUALITIES OF GOOD DISCUSSION QUESTIONS: A CHECKLIST FOR EVALUATING QUESTIONS

Any question that generates a lively discussion has several characteristics. It is clear, specific, and interpretive. It also has the vital element of doubt about the answer but is answerable on the basis of the story alone. Finally, it is a problem that the questioner cares about, that is, something that he or she really wants to solve. To avoid wasting discussion time, check your questions first to be sure that they have these six qualities. *In the order given,* use the questions on this checklist to evaluate your questions.

1. *Is my question clear?* Does my question make sense as written? Would I have to explain a word or phrase for someone who does not understand what I am getting at? If yes, mark your question NC for not clear and try to revise it if you can. If no, that is, if you think your question is clear, go on to the next step.
2. *Is my question specific?* Is my question so general that it could be asked of any story? Have I pinpointed a *problem* about meaning? If no, mark the question NS and try to revise it. If yes, that is, if your question can be asked only of this reading because it is tailor made, go on to the next step.
3. *Is my question interpretive?* Have I written a factual question? If yes, mark it NIF for not interpretive but factual and try to revise. Could I have written an evaluative question? If yes, mark NIE for not interpretive but evaluative and try to revise it. However, if there is more than one answer to my question, that is, if someone could disagree based on his or her reading of the story, go on to the next step.
4. *Does my question have the vital element of doubt about the answer?* Do I already have an answer to this question in mind? If yes, can I think of a second, equally plausible answer? If no, mark it LD for lacks doubt and try to revise by reviewing the three levels of doubt in writing interpretive questions. If you can think of no answer to your question, *or* if you can think of at least two equally good answers based on the text, go on to the next step.
5. *Is my question answerable on basis of the reading alone* or does t go outside the information given in the story? If no, mark it NA for not answerable and try to revise it. Note: do not conclude that if you can think of no answer to your question, you can dismiss it immediately as not answerable. You will learn in discussion whether or not if it is answerable. Finally,

6. *Do I care about getting an answer to this question in discussion?* If no, mark LC for lacks care and write a question that really bothers you and that you want to answer. If yes, mark your question GOOD because you know you have written a question that will generate a lively discussion that will increase your own and the groups' understanding and enjoyment of the reading.

GASTON LESSON PLAN 3: BASIC QUESTIONS

1. Focus	Why do some questions last longer in discussion than others? Some are basic and others are minor. Basic questions have multiple implications because they are about a major theme of the reading.
2. Objective (what):	To write questions that sustain discussion—those that deal with a major theme of the reading.
3. Purpose (why):	To obtain a more comprehensive understanding of the story than is likely when discussing a random list of prepared questions.
4. Input:	Review the handout on the four qualities of good basic questions.
5. Modeling:	Review one of the model basic questions on Gaston or The Road Not Taken.
6. Checking:	Review quiz with entire class. Peer grading.
7. Guided practice:	Review quiz with entire class. Peer grading.
8. Closure:	Again, when do you know if you have written a good basic question for discussion?

This lesson plan is set up for a 50-minute period. If you have a 90-minute period in a block schedule, you could extend the guided practice by putting students into groups of four and having them try to write their own basic question. In the beginning, this difficult task can be made easier by giving the class a basic question without any follow-ups.

ANSWER KEY FOR EXERCISE 1 ON BASIC QUESTIONS: *GASTON*

Basic Questions:

1. Why does the father let his daughter make up her own mind about which parent to live with instead of telling her what to do?
2. Does the author intend the little girl's situation to be like Gaston's?

Directions: For each question below, put a *1* in front of those related to the first basic question and a *2* in front of those that are related to the second.

__1__ 1. Why doesn't the father make plans with his daughter about what they would do?

__2__ 2. Are we to believe that the girl's home, like Gaston's, can never be in order again because of her parent's divorce?

__1__ 3. Why does the father answer with questions when his daughter asks if he is going to squash Gaston or holler?

__1__ 4. Why does the father let his daughter decide whether to go with him to buy a peach or to stay at home?

__2__ 5. Is the girl homeless in a sense because she is divided in her loyalty to her father and her mother?

__2__ 6. Why does everything seem wrong with Gaston just after the mother's phone call?

__2__ 7. Is the author suggesting that the girl, like Gaston, cannot live happily in her father's house?

__1__ 8. Why doesn't the father tell the girl what to say if her mother calls, except that he has gone to get her a bad peach?

__1__ 9. Why doesn't the father comment when his daughter says, "I want to be here"?

__2__ 10. Is the "break" in Gaston's house intended to suggest the break in the girl's life when her parents divorced?

__1__ 11. Why does the father ask his daughter why she squashed Gaston instead of scolding her?

__2__ 12. Why is Gaston wandering around confused after the mother's telephone call?

__2__ 13. If the little girl's situation is like Gaston's, why does the author have both her and her father say Gaston is like him?

__1__ 14. Why does the father resist his impulse to hug his daughter as she leaves?

__1__ 15. Why does the father say only "Oh" when his daughter says she is flying back to New York?

__2__ 16. Why does the girl's crying after she squashed Gaston remind her of when she cried "long ago"?

ANSWER KEY FOR EXERCISE 2 ON BASIC QUESTIONS: *GASTON*

Directions: Put an X next to any of the questions in the cluster of this basic question, that lack one of the six qualities of a good prepared discussion question. On a separate sheet of paper, revise or replace those questions that are not appropriate.

Why does Saroyan give the girl a mother and father who are so different?

_____ 1. Why does the author have the mother and father live in different countries?

_____ 2. Why does the mother call the insect a bug while the father gives it a name and a personality?

__X__ 3. Where does the father live? (FACT: Paris)

__X__ 4. Would you rather live with the little girl's mother or father?

_____ 5. Why does the mother try to persuade the girl to leave but the father not try to persuade her to stay?

__X__ 6. What is the main conflict in the story? (NS)

__X__ 7. Will the girl ever see her father again? (NA)

_____ 8. Why does the author have the mother send the chauffeur to pick up the girl instead of coming herself?

__X__ 9. Do the mother and father both have the best interest of the girl in mind? (AMBIGUOUS: According to who? Saroyan? (INT—OK) Your standards? (EVAL-X))

_____ 10. Why does the author have the father buy two kilo of peaches before he finds some with flaws in them?

_____ 11. At the end of the story why does the father feel somewhat like Gaston?

__X__ 12. How long have the girl's parents been divorced? (NA)

_____ 13. Why does the author have the mother appear to be richer than the father?

_____ 14. Unlike the father, why is the mother full of plans for her daughter?

__X__ 15. Why does only the insect have a name in the story? (NOT RELATED)

__X__ 16. To whom does the author compare the girl's father? (FACT)

GASTON LESSON PLAN 4: SPONTANEOUS FOLLOW-UP QUESTIONS

1. Focus:	During discussion how can you tell if the co-leaders are listening to your responses? They follow-up on your ideas with questions of clarification, substantiation, consistency, etc.
2. Objective (what):	To prepare co-leaders to ask good follow-up questions that are based on participant's responses. To learn how to develop participant's ideas in discussion. To anticipate some common problems that arise for co-leaders during discussion.
3. Purpose (why):	To anticipate and learn how to handle some common problems that arise for co-leaders during discussion.
4. Input:	Review exercise on spontaneous follow-up questions.
5. Modeling:	Review exercise on spontaneous follow-up questions.
6. Checking:	Review exercise with entire class.
7. Guided practice:	Review exercise with entire class.
8. Closure:	Review the kind and purpose of the seven types of spontaneous follow-up questions. (Handout follows)

This lesson plan is set up for a 50-minute period. If you have a 90-minute period in a block schedule, you could extend the guided practice by dividing the class into small groups of six and have them complete the Scenario Exercise. (Handout follows)

SEVEN KINDS OF SPONTANEOUS FOLLOW-UP QUESTIONS

There are several distinct kinds of follow-up questions that could be asked at any given moment of discussion. The kind of follow-up question asked in specific situation depends on the leader's purpose.

1. Is it *to clarify?* For example: "What did you mean when you said _____?" or "Could you explain more of what you mean by____?"
2. Is it *to substantiate?* For example: "Upon what in the reading are you basing your answer?" or "How do you know? What in the reading gave you that impression?"
3. Is it *to get more opinion?* For example: "Maria, do you agree with John's view that___? If so, could you explain? If not, why do you disagree?"
4. Is it *to test for consistency?* For example: "Sarah, if what you say is correct, how do you explain ___?"
5. Is it *to relate* a response to the prepared question? For example: "Brian, how does what you have just said help answer our question about___?"
6. Is it *to draw out the implications* of an answer? For example: "Ryan, are you then saying that____?" or "Would you then go so far as to say___?" or finally,
7. Is it *to resolve* the prepared question? For example: "John, at this moment, what is your best answer to our question about___? or "Laura, how many different answers have you heard so far to our basic question about____?"

ANSWER KEY FOR EXERCISE ON SPONTANEOUS FOLLOW-UP QUESTIONS ON *GASTON*

Directions: Each group below consists of a prepared question and a response given during discussion. After each response, write in what you consider to be a good follow-up question. Remember that the general purpose of any follow-up question (which can be factual, interpretive, or even evaluative) is to get the participant *to reflect* on his or her answer and *to develop* it.

1. Leader: Why does the mother try to persuade her daughter to leave but the father tell her only that the important thing is what she wants?

   Sarah: Because the mother is selfish and more involved with her own feelings. She doesn't even realize that it might be better for her daughter to live with her father. But I wonder why the girl wanted a rotten peach.

   Follow-up question: ______________________________

   Comment: How do you deal with several ideas in a response? Follow-up on any one of them. Do not ignore all of them (except those clearly irrelevant) and ask for another opinion. For example: "Sarah, how does the mother show she's involved in her own feelings?" (substantiation) or: "Linda, do you do you agree with Sarah that the mother is not concerned about having her daughter live with her father?" (more opinion).

2. Leader: Is the author implying that the girl's house, like Gaston's, can never be put in order again because of her parent's divorce?

   Brian: For sure. All the kids that I know whose parents have split are pretty unhappy people.

   Follow-up question: ______________________________

   Comment: The answer is evaluative, based on personal experience not the story. The solution is to turn Brian back into the story. For example: "Brian what in the story shows that the little girl is unhappy about her parent's divorce?"

3. Leader: Why does the father answer with questions when the girl asks if he is going to squash Gaston?

   Rachael: What questions?

	Follow-up question:	______________________________________
	Comment:	Failure to remember something in the story. Three options: (1) ask Rachael to look up the relevant passage; (2) ask someone else if they remember the questions; or (3) rephrase the question with one of the father's questions in it.
4.	Leader:	Near the end of the story, why does Saroyan refer to the father as "THE MAN"?
	John:	I don't have a clue. Call on somebody else. Anyway, who cares?
	Follow-up question:	______________________________________
	Comment:	No response at all (which is not uncommon in early discussions). Six options: (1) repeat the question to give the student time to think; (2) rephrase the question; (3) ask a related factual question; (4) ask a related interpretive question; (5) ask a related question of evaluation; or, finally, (6) call on another student.
5.	Leader:	Why does the father resist the impulse to hug his daughter when she leaves to return to her mother?
	Laura:	He really doesn't love her at all. She was just something he got rid of.
	Follow-up question:	______________________________________
	Comment:	A wrong answer, that is, an interpretation that cannot be supported by the evidence or which is contradicted by other evidence. Options: (1) ask for the supporting evidence that the father doesn't love his daughter; (2) ask someone else if they agree; (If they agree, ask them for their evidence;) (3) ask a follow-up question for consistency to introduce the contradictory evidence; (For example, "Laura, if the father doesn't love his daughter why does he tell her that the important thing is that she chooses where she wants to live?"). The leader must not tell the student that he or she is wrong. Participants must learn to judge for themselves which answers are right or wrong.
6.	Leader:	Why does the mother ridicule the girl's father but he say nothing bad about the mother?
	Chris:	Because that's what the story is all about.

Follow-up question: ________________________________

Comment: The reply is undeveloped and vague. Three options: (1) ask for clarification: "Chris, what is the story 'all about'?"; (2) get another opinion; or (3) ask for implications: "Chris, do you mean the story is all about the struggle between the mother and the father for control?"

7. Leader: Why does no one in the story have a name except for Gaston?

Participant: Her father wants to be entertaining. He's a fun kinda guy.

Follow-up question: ________________________________

Comment: Follow up on either idea but do not ignore them both.

8. Leader: Why does the girl ask her father why it is important for her to be where she wants to be?

Linda: I'll bet that question never occurred to her as being important before that moment.

Marc: She's probably so confused by this time that she really doesn't understand her situation.

David: Maybe she wants to see if her father would react like her mother. She did ask him what she should say if her mother called when he was gone.

Follow-up question: ________________________________

Comment: Multiple, rapid responses. What do the co-leaders do? Three options: (1) Follow-up on any one of the answers but do not ignore them all and merely call on another participant. Which one do you pursue? Pursue whichever one seems the most interesting or relevant to you. (2) Table one or two responses on your seating chart that you do not immediately pursue and come back to them later in discussion. (3) Ask Linda or Marc if he or she agrees with David's interpretation.

SOCRATIC SEMINAR SCENARIO EXERCISE

Co-leaders: (1) ______________________ (2) ______________________
Group members: (1) ______________________ (2) ______________________
(3) ______________________ (4) ______________________

1. Co-leaders' prepared question: ______________________________
____

2. Your answer: ______________________________________
____

   Write down answers offered by other group members:
   A1 __________: ______________________________
   (name)
   ____
   A2 __________: ______________________________
   (name)
   ____
   Write down your follow-up question: ______________________
   ____
   Write down the follow-up question chosen by the leader: __________
   ____

3. Write down your answer: ______________________________
____

   Write down answers offered by other group members:
   A1 __________: ______________________________
   (name)
   ____
   A2 __________: ______________________________
   (name)
   ____
   Write down your follow-up question: ______________________
   ____

4. Write down your answer: ______________________________
____

   Write down answers offered by other group members:
   A1 __________: ______________________________
   (name)

____

A2 ________: _______________
(name)

____

Write down your follow-up question: _______________

____

Write down the follow-up question chosen by the leader: ________

____

5. Write down your answer: _______________

____

Write down answers offered by other group members:

A1 ________: _______________
(name)

____

A2 ________: _______________
(name)

____

Write down your follow-up question: _______________

____

6. Write down your answer: _______________

____

Write down answers offered by other group members:

A1________: _______________
(name)

____

A2________: _______________
(name)

____

Write down your follow-up question: _______________

____

Conclusion: After recording six sequences, review with your class the leader's choice of follow-up questions: What kind of follow-up was asked? What was its purpose? Was it related to the participant's answer? Did it keep the prepared (focus) question in sight?

GASTON LESSON PLAN 5: PREPARING CO-LEADERS FOR DISCUSSION

1. Focus:	What questions do you have at this moment about co-leading a discussion yourself next week?
2. Objective (what):	To answer all your questions about co-leading. To dispel your doubts about co-leading. To develop your confidence as a co-leader.
3. Purpose (why):	To prepare you to be effective co-leaders so that we all will increase our mutual understanding and enjoyment of the assigned readings.
4. Input:	Review the four rules of Socratic discussion (see Figure 3.2, p. 30). Review the Guidelines for Co-leading (p. 80). Review the Use of the Seating Chart (p. 81). Review Criteria for Critique of Discussion (p. 82). Review Guidelines for Preparing Discussion Questions (p. 83).
5. Modeling:	Conduct a 20-minute demonstration discussion with a student co-leader on a short reading (e.g., a poem).
6. Checking:	Review the demonstration discussion by having students raise questions about how the ten criteria were or were not applied.
7. Guided practice:	Review the demonstration discussion by having students raise questions about how each of the ten criteria were or were not followed.
8. Closure:	Have all your questions about co-leading been answered to your satisfaction?

This lesson plan is set up for a 50-minute period. If you have a 90-minute period in a block schedule, you could extend modeling by conducting a 30-minute demonstration discussion in which you explain why you are asking each follow-up question as you go along.

GUIDELINES FOR CO-LEADING A SOCRATIC DISCUSSION

When you co-lead a 15-minute discussion of an assigned reading, please follow these guidelines to insure that discussion is truly Socratic.

1. Sit next to your co-leader and make out a seating chart from your position in the group.
2. Have the group write down your prepared question, basic or otherwise, on a piece of paper and give them about three minutes to jot down a brief, initial response.
3. The leaders and the group must observe the four rules of discussion:
   - No one may participate who has not read the text;
   - Discuss only the text that everyone has read;
   - *The co-leaders may only ask questions, they must avoid statements of any kind;* and
   - Do not bring in an outside authority to support your answers. Rely on the text for evidence.
4. Begin the discussion by calling on someone by name to give his or her answer. Address all participants by name to control the flow of discussion. Although participants may speak up freely without being called upon, the co-leaders must recognize them by name to direct the group's attention.
5. Make every effort to call on everyone in your group at least once or twice. Put a mark next to the name on your seating chart every time that you call on someone to respond. *Avoid the extremes of calling on the same few participants too often or of not calling on someone at all.*
6. For every two or three responses, you and your co-leader should be asking a spontaneous follow-up question to develop the ideas given and to keep the group's thinking focused on your prepared question.
7. At the end of 15–20 minutes, ask individuals in the group to recall briefly the different answers that have been given to your prepared question. Note these answers briefly on your seating chart and hand it in at the end of class.
8. The answers to your prepared question noted on your seating chart are the degree to which you have increased your own and the group's understanding of the reading (the goal of shared inquiry). This is the resolution of discussion; it is an individual matter, *not* a group consensus.

THE USE AND IMPORTANCE OF THE SEATING CHART

At the beginning of each discussion, it is important that the co-leaders make a seating chart from their position in the group that is seated in a circle. The seating chart has three important functions:

1. It locates each participant and enables you to call on each person by name. Preface all your questions by name.
   - This helps you to control the discussion.
   - If all have responsibility for a question, usually none do.
   - It gives the person called on a few seconds to think of an answer. In theory, everyone should be prepared to speak all the time, but in practice, it seldom works out that way.
   - It enables you to invite those less likely to speak up on their own. Throwing a question out to everyone usually results in the verbally aggressive taking over.
2. It enables the co-leaders to involve all participants more or less equally.
   - During a 15- to 30-minute segment of discussion, the co-leaders should try to call on everyone at least once, ideally twice.
   - The co-leaders should ask an average of one follow-up question for every two or three responses.
3. It enables the co-leaders to exercise their three options: to ignore, to table, or to pursue responses.
   - Next to the names of participants, the co-leaders can jot down those ideas they are pursuing immediately and to table those for later discussion.
   - Because it is impossible to follow-up on every idea in discussion, the co-leaders must make conscious choices about what they pursue immediately, table for later, or ignore. Unless they do so, they will begin to *tag end*—to pick up on the last remark of the last participant. When this happens, discussion degenerates into a series of unrelated comments.

CRITERIA FOR CRITIQUE OF SOCRATIC DISCUSSION: A CHECKLIST

Co-leaders ______________ and ______________ English ________

Reading ______________________________________ Date ___________

Question ____

Code: Good (10) Pretty good (5) Needs improvement (0)

1. Did the leaders initiate discussion by beginning with a *good interpretive question*?

   10 5 0

2. Did the leaders call on *all* participants at least once?

   10 5 0

3. Did the leaders *average* one follow-up question for every two or three responses?

   10 5 0

4. Did the leaders *avoid making statements* or asking leading questions?

   10 5 0

5. Did the leaders seek *clarification* as well as *substantiation* when necessary?

   10 5 0

6. Did the leaders *co-lead*? Did they share equally the task of asking follow-up questions?

   10 5 0

7. Did the leaders get answers to *questions on the floor* before moving on to new ideas?

   10 5 0

8. Did the leaders *stick to* their prepared question?

   10 5 0

9. Did the leaders *pick up* ideas from the participants for follow-up questions or, if they began with a basic question, did they rely too much on their list of prepared follow-up questions?

   10 5 0

10. Did the leaders *resolve* their prepared question?

    10 5 0

TOTALS: (___/100)

GUIDELINES FOR PRE-DISCUSSION: PREPARING DISCUSSION QUESTIONS WITH YOUR CO-LEADER

1. Before meeting with your co-leader, each of you should have written fifteen or twenty interpretive questions with a page reference for each whenever possible. The page references will make it easy for both of you to turn to the page that gave you the idea for the question. Page references also help you to make your questions specific.
2. Begin pre-discussion by checking the wording of your questions. Do this by applying the Checklist for Qualities of Good Discussion Questions (handout in *Gaston* Lesson Plan 2, p. 64). If you cannot revise your questions to have these six characteristics, drop them. If you have trouble getting to your deepest level of understanding (that is, writing questions that have real doubt for you) review the handout on the Three Levels of Doubt (*Gaston* Lesson Plan 2, p. 65).
3. At this point, you should decide if you want to go with a list of at least 10 good interpretive questions (arranged in any order that seems logical to you) or decide on writing a basic question similar to those that accompany the lesson plan for each reading. Indeed, you may want to try out one of the suggested basic questions that lack follow-up questions and see if together you can come up with a cluster of at least eight interpretive follow-up questions.
4. Agree upon the question that you want to use to open your discussion. Do not be overly concerned with your choice of an opening question. Any question that you both genuinely care about will be suitable.

TWO IMPORTANT CAVEATS

- If you do not have pre-discussion with your co-leader before each discussion meeting, you cannot expect to have even a reasonably good experience. In failing to carry out your responsibility to the group, you will also be failing yourselves. If you enjoy co-leading and want to increase your skill to become a good discussion leader who turns students on to reading and learning from one another, pre-discussion is imperative.
- The model basic questions that accompany the Lesson Plan for each reading are *not* intended to be ready-made questions that you can try out on a group. The issues they raise, the questions they pose, are meant to make you think harder and better about *your own questions*.

To be sure, next to asking good spontaneous follow-up questions, the hardest part of the Socratic method is coming up with your own questions about the readings. Why? Because there are no answer keys for discussion and because thinking *is* difficult! Nevertheless, its rewards are great.

6

LESSON PLANS

INDEX OF LESSON PLANS

LESSON PLAN 1: *THE CHOCOLATE WAR*

1. Focus:	What is your biggest problem in high school? (5 minutes)
2. Objective:	To solve several questions of interpretation about the overall meaning of the novel.
3. Purpose:	To increase our mutual understanding (comprehension) and, as a result, our enjoyment of the story. To develop the habit of independent and critical thinking.
4. Input:	Begin with a factual quiz to check that everyone has read the novel. (Rule 1: No one may participate who has not read the selection.) The quiz should be ten factual questions, short answers (not True/False). Those with 70% are in the inner circle; those with less are in the outer circle. (15 minutes)
	Four basic questions (pp. 89–90). (60 minutes)
5. Modeling, checking, and guided practice:	During discussion the co-leaders model the four rules of discussion, and check for understanding by asking follow-up questions for clarification, substantiation, consistency, relevance, implication, resolution, and to get more opinion. Guided practice is the discussion.
6. Closure:	Oral or written resolution of one or two basic questions just discussed. How would you have tried to help Jerry cope with high school?

During Socratic Seminar day(s), in a full 90-minute period, four pairs of student co-leaders each lead a 15-minute discussion of the reading. It is important that the teacher approves the student co-leaders' questions before discussion to avoid wasting time on questions that are not clear, are factual, or evaluative. (Discussion should center on solving problems, not on trying to figure out what the problems are.) During the remaining time (if any) the teacher leads a demonstration discussion (modeling) of one of his or her basic questions on the reading of the lesson.

TEXT: Cormier, R. (1974). *The Chocolate War.* New York: Bantam Doubleday Dell Books.

BASIC QUESTION FOR *THE CHOCOLATE WAR*

Why does Jerry Renault refuse to participate in the annual school fund-raiser?

1. Does Jerry want a confrontation with Brother Leon? (p. 38)
2. Does Jerry honestly believe that participation is voluntary? (p. 66)
3. Why does the narrator ask if Jerry is defying Brother Leon and the Trinity sale tradition? (p. 67)
4. Why can't Brian Cockran, treasurer of the chocolate sale, understand Jerry's refusal? (p. 76)
5. Why do some student's think that Jerry's defiance is a Vigil assignment? (p. 88)
6. Why does Jerry admit that he had not planned to refuse to sell? (p. 91)
7. Why does Jerry disagree with the student who thought his refusal to sell was "cool"? (p. 95)
8. What connection does Jerry see between the poster in his locker and his decision not to sell? (pp. 97, 142, 164, 187)
9. Why can't Jerry explain to the Vigils his motive for not selling? (p. 124)
10. Does Jerry's motive change? (p. 124)
11. Why does Jerry refuse the Vigil assignment to sell chocolates? (p. 126)

SOME ALTERNATIVE BASIC QUESTIONS

Here are three more basic questions that you can qualify for discussion if you can come up with at least eight related interpretive follow-up questions for each. When students are struggling to write their own basic questions, I sometimes give them a basic question as an intermediate step to writing their own clusters. They then have to come up with at least eight related interpretive follow-up questions of their own.

BASIC QUESTION NO. 2

According to Cormier, is Archie Costello basically right about us all being "bastards" (greedy and cruel)? (p. 175) Rephrased: *Is the author suggesting that it is not possible to be true to one's self?*

BASIC QUESTION NO. 3

Does Cormier want us to agree with Goober that Trinity High School is an evil place? (pp. 87, 116)

BASIC QUESTION NO. 4

Why does Cormier portray the Headmaster, Brother Leon, as a sadistic hypocrite?

CAVEAT

The model basic questions that accompany the Lesson Plan for each reading are *not* intended to be ready-made questions that you can try out on a group. The issues they raise, the questions they pose, are meant to make you think harder and better about *your own* questions. To be sure, next to asking good spontaneous follow-up questions, the hardest part of the Socratic method is coming up with your own questions about the readings. Why? There are no answer keys for discussion and because thinking is difficult! Nevertheless, the rewards are great.

LESSON PLAN 2:
BEYOND THE CHOCOLATE WAR

1. Focus:	What is your biggest problem in high school? (5 minutes)
2. Objective:	To solve several questions of interpretation about the overall meaning of the novel.
3. Purpose:	To increase our mutual understanding (comprehension) and, as a result, our enjoyment of the story. To develop the habit of independent and critical thinking.
4. Input:	Begin with a factual quiz to check that everyone has read the novel. (Rule 1: No one may participate who has not read the selection.) The quiz should be ten factual questions, short answers (not True/False). Those with 70% are in the inner circle; those with less are in the outer circle. (15 minutes)
	Two or four basic questions. Handout follows. (30 or 60 minutes)
5. Modeling, checking, and guided practice:	During discussion the co-leaders model the four rules of discussion, and check for understanding by asking follow-up questions for clarification, substantiation, consistency, relevance, implication, resolution, and to get more opinion. Guided practice is the discussion.
6. Closure:	Oral or written resolution of one or two basic questions just discussed. How would you have tried to help Jerry cope with high school?

During Socratic Seminar day(s), in a full 90-minute period, four pairs of student co-leaders each lead a 15-minute discussion of the reading. It is important that the teacher approves the student co-leaders' questions before discussion to avoid wasting time on questions that are not clear, are factual, or evaluative. (Discussion should center on solving problems, not on trying to figure out what the problems are.) During the remaining time (if any) the teacher leads a demonstration discussion (modeling) of one of his or her basic questions on the reading of the lesson.

TEXT: Cormier, R. (1985) *Beyond Chocolate War.* New York: Bantam Doubleday Dell Books.

BASIC QUESTION FOR *BEYOND THE CHOCOLATE WAR*

Why does Archie Costello have such a cynical attitude towards life?

1. Is Archie an atheist? (p. 44)
2. Because "nobody's perfect" according to Archie, why is he so revulsed by Brother Leon's hypocrisy? (pp. 45, 145)
3. How did Archie discover "the secret of the world's agony"? (p. 45)
4. Why does Archie say "everyone loves the smell of his own shit"? (p. 69)
5. Why does Archie always look for ways to exploit people? (p. 145)
6. When Morton (Jill) tells Archie that he always "makes people feel like shit," why does Archie tell her to blame human nature? (p. 145)
7. Because Archie believes that everyone has faults, does he see no goodness at all in human nature? (p. 145)
8. Why doesn't Archie want anyone to get close to him? (p. 147)
9. Since he doesn't study, why is Archie able to get passing grades? (p. 204)
10. Why doesn't Archie seem to love anybody or anything, according to Obie? (p. 205)
11. Does the author imply that Archie lacks normal, human feelings? (p. 205)
12. Given his cynical attitude towards life, why doesn't Archie regard himself as evil or as a looser? (p. 262)

SOME ALTERNATIVE BASIC QUESTIONS

Here are three more basic questions that you can qualify for discussion if you can come up with at least eight related interpretive follow-up questions for each. When students are struggling to write their own basic questions, I sometimes give them a basic question as an intermediate step to writing their own clusters. They then have to come up with at least eight related interpretive follow-up questions of their own.

BASIC QUESTION NO. 2

Does Cormier want us to agree with Archie Costello that everyone, but not him, made Trinity High School corrupt?

BASIC QUESTION NO. 3

Why does the story end with the election of Henry Malloran as senior class president and Ray Bunting and Emile Janza making plans for the next school year?

BASIC QUESTION NO. 4

Why are some of the characters so disgusted at their willingness to follow Archie?

CAVEAT

The model basic questions that accompany the Lesson Plan for each reading are *not* intended to be ready-made questions that you can try out on a group. The issues they raise, the questions they pose, are meant to make you think harder and better about *your own* questions. To be sure, next to asking good spontaneous follow-up questions, the hardest part of the Socratic method is coming up with your own questions about the readings. Why? There are no answer keys for discussion and because thinking is difficult! Nevertheless, the rewards are great.

LESSON PLAN 3: *THE GIVER*

1. Focus:	How would you like to live in a world of complete security where you did not have to worry about anything? (5 minutes)
2. Objective:	To solve several questions of interpretation about the overall meaning of the novel.
3. Purpose:	To increase our mutual understanding (comprehension) and, as a result, our enjoyment of the story. To develop the habit of independent and critical thinking.
4. Input:	Begin with a factual quiz to check that everyone has read the novel. (Rule 1: No one may participate who has not read the selection.) The quiz should be ten factual questions, short answers (not True/False). Those with 70% are in the inner circle; those with less are in the outer circle. (15 minutes)
	Two or four basic questions (pp. 95–97). (30 or 60 minutes)
5. Modeling, checking, and guided practice:	During discussion the co-leaders model the four rules of discussion, and check for understanding by asking follow-up questions for clarification, substantiation, consistency, relevance, implication, resolution, and to get more opinion. Guided practice is the discussion.
6. Closure:	Oral or written resolution of one or two basic questions just discussed. When is the price of security too high?

During Socratic Seminar day(s), in a full 90-minute period, four pairs of student co-leaders each lead a 15-minute discussion of the reading. It is important that the teacher approves the student co-leaders' questions before discussion to avoid wasting time on questions that are not clear, are factual, or evaluative. (Discussion should center on solving problems, not on trying to figure out what the problems are.) During the remaining time (if any) the teacher leads a demonstration discussion (modeling) of one of his or her basic questions on the reading of the lesson.

TEXT: Lowry, L. (1993). *The Giver.* New York: Bantam Doubleday Dell Books.

BASIC QUESTION FOR *THE GIVER*

How did people in the world of Sameness forget that they were human?

1. What is the purpose of the daily family ritual of sharing feelings? (pp. 4–6)
2. Why do people not prepare their own meals?
3. Why have sexual feelings ("stirrings") been suppressed in the world of Sameness? (pp. 37, 129)
4. Why are children assigned to families rather than born into them? (p. 42)
5. Why is precision of language one of the most important tasks for children to learn? (p. 55)
6. Why does the world of Sameness need a Giver and a Receiver of Memory? (p. 64)
7. Why is The Receiver's Assignment the most important of all? (p. 67)
8. How has the world of Sameness been able to endure for so many generations? (p. 77)
9. Why is any one allowed to take medication for pain? (p. 69)
10. Does using "precise language" mean being literal? (pp. 70, 71, 75, 89)
11. Why are there no books other than those needed for daily routine? (p. 74)
12. Why had color, hills, and intemperate weather been eliminated? (pp. 83–85)
13. Does language define or reflect experience in the world of Sameness? (pp. 89, 95)
14. Why is the school curriculum limited to language and communications, commerce and industry, science and technology, and civil procedures and government? (p. 89)
15. Why is there but one Receiver of Memories?
16. Why is there no mention of God or belief in Transcendence in this community?
17. Why do the people find memories of any kind so painful?

18. How had the world of Sameness been able to isolate itself from other communities?
19. Why is it inappropriate to use the word love in the community? (pp. 127–128)
20. What does The Giver mean when he tells Jonas that people *"know nothing"*? (p. 153)
21. Does the last sentence of the story mean that Jonas had forgotten what music was? (p. 180)

SOME ALTERNATIVE BASIC QUESTIONS

Here are three more basic questions that you can qualify for discussion if you can come up with at least eight related interpretive follow-up questions for each. When students are struggling to write their own basic questions, I sometimes give them a basic question as an intermediate step to writing their own clusters. They then have to develop at least eight of their own related interpretive follow-up questions.

BASIC QUESTION NO. 2

Does Lois Lowry want us to regard The Giver as heroic?

BASIC QUESTION NO. 3

Does Lowry intend Jonas to be a Christ figure?

BASIC QUESTION NO. 4

Why are there so many rules in the world of Sameness?

CAVEAT

The model basic questions that accompany the Lesson Plan for each reading are *not* intended to be ready-made questions that you can try out on a group. The issues they raise, the questions they pose, are meant to make you think harder and better about *your own* questions. To be sure, next to asking good spontaneous follow-up questions, the hardest part of the Socratic method is coming up with your own questions about the readings. Why? There are no answer keys for discussion and because thinking is difficult! Nevertheless, the rewards are great.

LESSON PLAN NO. 4: *SHANE*

Lesson 1:	View film version of novel and complete Notation Sheet number 1. Handout follows.
Lesson 2:	Complete Notation Sheet number 2 and discuss differences. Handout follows.
Lesson 3:	What is Schaefer's idea of a code hero (a man)? This lesson plan.
Lesson 4:	Essay Exam on Shane. Handout follows.

1. Focus:	Journal writing: What is your definition of a man? (5 minutes)
2. Objective:	To solve a basic question of interpretation about Schaefer's definition of a code hero—a man.
3. Purpose:	To increase our mutual understanding (comprehension) and, as a result, our enjoyment of the story. To develop the habit of independent and critical thinking.
4. Input:	Begin with a factual quiz to check that everyone has read the novel. (Rule 1: No one may participate who has not read the selection.) The quiz should be ten factual questions, short answers (not True/False). Those with 70% are in the inner circle; those with less are in the outer circle. (20 minutes)
5. Modeling, and checking	During discussion the co-leaders model the four rules of discussion, and check for understanding by asking follow-up questions for clarification, substantiation, consistency, relevance, implication, resolution, and to get more opinion. Basic question: What is a man, according to Schaefer?
6. Guided practice:	Review the handout on The Code Hero in Shane which follows.
7. Closure:	A formal essay on the qualities the Schaefer believes are needed for a code hero and a personal assessment about their personal value to the student.

TEXT: Schaefer, J. (1949). *Shane.* New York: Bantam Books.

DISCUSSION GUIDE FOR SCHAEFER'S CODE HERO IN *SHANE*: WHAT IS A MAN?

Directions: In *Shane*, Schaefer uses the word *man* more than 100 times. Nearly always, the word refers to more than a male. (1) Look up the context of each of the following quotations on the pages given and *identify the speaker.* (2) Beneath each quotation, write *a synonym or phrase* that could be put in place of the word *man.* (3) From these quotations, make a *list of qualities* needed for a Schaefer code hero.

1. "A man who watches what's going on around him will make his mark." (p. 5)

2. "I don't think you ever had a safer man in your house." (p. 9)

3. "A man has to pay his debts." (p. 17)

4. "We started this with man power and we'll finish it with man power." (p. 26)

5. "This job is too big for one man, even for me." (p. 32)

6. "We've got ourselves a man." (p. 33)

7. "What a man knows isn't important. It's what he is that counts." (p. 33)

8. "He knows I'm in a spot and he's not the man to leave me there.... He's my kind of man." (p. 33)

9. "I've never met a man I'd rather have more on my side in any kind of trouble." (p. 35)

10. "Why should a man refuse to wear a gun and show it off?" (p. 38)

11. "There are some things you don't ask a man." (p. 38)

12. "A man like Shane." (p. 38)

13. "A gun is as good—and as bad as the man who carries it." (p. 44)

14. "Why should a man be smashed because he has courage and does what he's told?" (p. 54)

15. "Take good care of him. He has the makings of a good man." (p. 62)

16. "In my opinion, Shane was the most dangerous man I've ever seen." (pp. 62, 102)

17. "A man can keep his self respect without having to cram it down another man's throat." (p. 64)

18. "He could have called it off without crawling. He could have if he was man enough." (p. 64)

19. "I know you're the man to stand up to it." (p. 66)

20. "I'm man enough to know a better man when his trail meets mine." (p. 80)

21. "There are some things a man can't take. Not if he's to go on living with himself." (p. 91)

22. "What better reason could a man have?" (p. 98)

23. "It helps a man to know that if anything happens to him, his family will be in better hands than his own" (p. 100)

24. "Tell him no man need be ashamed of being beat by Shane." (p. 103)

25. "No. Could I separate you in my mind and still be a man?" (p. 104)

26. "It's a lovely land, Bob. A good place to be a boy and grow straight inside as a man should." (p. 106)

27. "A man is what he is, Bob, and there's no breaking the mold. I tried that and I've lost." (p. 113)

28. "But I reckon it was in the cards from the moment I saw a freckled kid on a rail up the road there and a real man behind him, the kind that could back him for a chance another kid never had." (p. 113)

MOVIE NOTATION SHEET 1 FOR *SHANE*: MOVIE VS. NOVEL

Directions: List five important scenes in each column.

Retained	*Omitted*	*Added*

MOVIE NOTATION SHEET 2 FOR *SHANE*: MOVIE VS. NOVEL

Directions: Using Movie Notation Sheet 1, list five important scenes in each column. Write each as one complete sentence. Put them in chronological order with chapter number in parentheses.

Retained	*Omitted*	*Added*
	1. Shane first appears dressed entirely in black wearing no gun (Ch. 1)	1. Shane first appears in rawhide wearing a gun. (Ch. 1)
	2. Jake Ledyard does not try to sell Joe an over-priced cultivator. (Ch. 2)	
1. Shane and Joe's battle with the monster stump impresses both Marian and Bob. (Ch. 3)	3. Marian's hat and pie incident is omitted. (Ch. 3)	
	4. Shane carried no gun. (Ch. 4, p. 36)	2. When Shane is teaching Bob how to draw, he displays his marksmanship by shooting a small rock several times.
		3. This scene ends when Marian tells Shane that guns will have no place in her son's life.
	5. Shane tells Marian, not Bob, that a gun is a tool like any other tool (Ch 5, p. 44).	

(Continues on next page)

	6. "The way I'm telling you is as good as any and better than most" (Ch. 4., p. 43)	
	7. Ernie Wright, "the weakest" of the farmers is omitted. (Ch. 6, p. 47)	
		4. Frank Torrey is transformed into a hot-tempered Civil War veteran from the South.
2. Chris, a Fletcher henchman, is known for his "gay manner and reckless cour-age" (Ch. 6, p. 51)		

ESSAY EXAM FOR *SHANE*

Directions: Choose *one* topic. Write a well-organized essay of *at least a page and a half* on the paper provided. Put the *topic's letter* at the top of the paper and give your essay a *title* that hints at your thesis. *Begin with a thesis;* do not write an introduction. Use *third person* (no you or I, we or us) and *avoid slang and contractions.* Number each sentence, write on both sides of the paper, and do not skip lines. Keep verbs in the same tense (past or present but not both). Quotations from the novel must have a page reference. Put the page number in parentheses at the end of the quotation. *Before you hand in your paper, check for run-on sentences and fragments. Write in ink, no pencil ever.*

TOPICS

A. *What IS a real man?* Throughout the novel, Schaefer uses the word *man* over a hundred times. Nearly always, the word refers to *more than a male.* Using your list of 28 quotations from the novel which we reviewed and discussed in class, list at least *four* specific qualities that make a male a man. For each characteristic:

   1. Cite the quotation first.
   2. Explain what the word *man* means in the context of the quotation, andthen,
   3. Illustrate that quality with a specific example from the novel.

B. *How good is the movie version of Jack's Schaefer's novel?* Consult your two movie notation sheets and consider the nine questions below. *Select at least four* (circle the number of each) and then organize your answers to them into an essay of at least a page and a half.

   1. In what specific ways does the movie *not* emphasize the "peculiar", "dangerous," and "mysterious" elements of Shane's character?
   2. What effect does omitting the Jake Ledyard scene early in the novel (Ch. 2) have on Shane and Joe's relationship?
   3. Is Bob's (Joey's) admiration of Shane as great in the movie as it is in the novel?
   4. Does the movie measure up to the novel in revealing the mutual respect that Shane and Joe Starrett have for one another?

5. Is the movie as effective as the novel in showing how the mutual respect between Shane and Joe grows deeper as the story develops?
6. Is the movie as successful as the novel in portraying the subtle and delicate relationship between Shane and Marian Starrett?
7. Does the novel portray Shane' s relationship with the homesteaders in the same way that the novel does?
8. Is the conversion or transformation of Chris as believable in the movie as it is in the novel?
9. Is the theme of Shane's attempt to abandon his past as a gun fighter as evident in the movie as it is in the novel?

LESSON PLAN 5: *OF MICE AND MEN* (FOUR-DAY UNIT)

Lesson 1:	Plot-check quiz Ch. 1–2. Discussion of responses to chapters 1 and 2 questions. Film version of chapters 1 and 2. Handouts follow.
Lesson 2:	Plot-check quiz Ch. 3–4. Discussion of responses to chapters 3 and 4 questions. Film version of chapters 3 and 4. Handouts follow.
Lesson 3:	Plot-check quiz Ch. 5–6. Discussion of responses to chapters 5 and 6 questions. Film version of chapters 5 and 6. Handouts follow.
Lesson 4:	Seminar on the American dream—this lesson. Handouts follow.

1. Focus:	Trivia quiz on the American dream (p. 118). (10 minutes)
2. Objective:	To solve several questions of interpretation about the overall meaning of the novel.
3. Purpose:	To increase our mutual understanding (comprehension) and, as a result, our enjoyment of the story. To develop the habit of independent and critical thinking.
4. Input:	Twobasic questions (pp. 121–122). (30 or 60 minutes)
5. Modeling, checking, and guided practice:	During discussion the co-leaders model the four rules of discussion, and check for understanding by asking follow-up questions for clarification, substantiation, consistency, relevance, implication, resolution, and to get more opinion. Guided practice is the discussion.
6. Closure:	Oral or written resolution of one or two basic questions just discussed.

During Socratic Seminar day(s), in a full 90-minute period, four pairs of student co-leaders each lead a 15-minute discussion of the reading. It is important that the teacher approves the student co-leaders' questions before discussion to avoid wasting time on questions that are not clear, are factual, or evaluative. (Discussion should center on solving problems, not on trying to figure out what the problems are.) During the remaining time (if any) the teacher leads a demonstration discussion (modeling) of one of his or her basic questions on the reading of the lesson.

TEXT: Steinbeck, J. (1955). *Of Mice and Men*. New York: Bantam Books.

EXERCISE ON WRITTEN RESPONSES IN SHORT PARAGRAPHS FOR *OF MICE AND MEN*

DIRECTIONS:

1. On your own paper (no spiral) respond to these questions in *complete*, error-free, sentences.
2. Write a paragraph of at least five or six sentences for *each* question. Put a number in front of each sentence.
3. Skip two lines between each paragraph and number each paragraph with its question number.
4. *Do not read ahead.* Answer these questions as soon as possible after you have finished reading the corresponding chapters, while your reactions are still fresh in your mind.

CHAPTER 1

1. What is your personal reaction to the relationship between George and Lennie? How would you describe or explain it to someone who has not read the story?
2. Given George and Lennie's relationship, what prediction(s) can you make about how they will get along in their new job?

CHAPTER 2

3. What is your personal reaction to Curley, to the boss's son? To Curley's wife? To Slim? To Candy? Be as specific as possible with each person.
4. Do you sense any tension between any of these characters? If yes, why? If not, why not? What do you think will happen next in the story?

CHAPTER 3

5. What is your reaction to the killing of Candy's dog?
6. Why did Candy feel that he should have killed the dog himself?
7. What was your reaction to the fight between Curley and Lennie?
8. Will this fight lead to more trouble for Lennie and George? If yes, how do you know? If no, why not?

CHAPTER 4

9. Why is Crooks so lonely? What is his dream?
10. What is George and Lennie's dream?
11. What is Candy's dream?
12. Why did Crooks change his mind so quickly about wanting to join George and Lennie?
13. If someone called you a "dreamer," would you take it as an insult or as a compliment? *Explain.*

CHAPTER 5

14. What was your reaction to the death of Curley's wife?
15. How did your reaction to her death compare with Candy's? With George's? With Curley's? How do you explain the differences?
16. Who, if anyone, is to blame for the death of Curley's wife?
17. What alternatives do George and Lennie now have at this point in the story?

CHAPTER 6

18. Did Lennie's death shock you? If yes, why? If not, what was your reaction when George killed Lennie?
19. Does Steinbeck want you to believe that George made the right decision to kill Lennie? How do you know? What is your evidence from the story?
20. Why does the story end with Carlson asking Curley, "Now what the hell ya suppose is eatin' them two guys?"

PLOT-CHECK QUIZ ON *OF MICE AND MEN*: CHAPTERS 1 AND 2

Directions: These answers may be used once, more than once, or not at all because some are false and not all answers have been included. Sometimes you must provide your own answers. Put answers on your own paper, *not* on this quiz.

- John Steinbeck
- George Milton
- Lennie Small
- Carlson
- Candy
- Curley
- Curley's wife
- The boss
- Slim
- Crooks
- He was caught stealing rabbits.
- "I don' like this place...This ain't no good place. I wanna get outa here."
- He wanted to touch a girl's dress and to pet it like a mouse.
- To own a little farm, raise rabbits, and live "off the fatta the lan'."
- "If I was a relative of yours, I'd shoot myself."
- "When are we gonna get there?"
- To begin a new life in California.
- To go to Alaska for gold.

He (1) was not "real bright"—in fact, he was retarded. He was a very large man who had the mind of a child and loved to pet soft, furry, things.

He (2) was a farm hand who had assumed the responsibility of taking care of another, unrelated, farm hand who kept getting into trouble.

He (3) was an old, crippled farm hand who had an old, lame sheepdog for a pet.

He (4) was a small, cocky, arrogant man who was a bully and a former boxer.

He (5) was a tall, sympathetic farm hand who befriended George and Lennie. His word was law.

He (6) was "a pretty nice fella" who thought that George would probably steal Lennie's pay because he would not allow Lennie to speak for himself.

He (7) reprimanded this person (8) for staring at this person (9) who he also described as "jail bait," a "rat trap," and a "tart."

After the provocative appearance of this person (10), Lennie told George (11).

This (12) was the dream or plan of (13) and (14).

He (15) got into trouble in northern California (Weed) because he had (16).

He (17) was a powerful, big-stomached man who hated dogs.

He (18) was the stable buck who had been kicked by a horse. He read a lot.

He (19) repeatedly reminded him (20) that if he ever got into trouble, he was to hide in (21).

He (22) told him (23), "I got you to look after me, and you got me to look after you."

He (24) told George, "Ain't many guys travel around together...I don't know why."

George emphatically told Lennie to stay away from (25) and (26) because they could get them fired.

He (27) thought that he would probably have to "tangle" with him (28) sooner or later because (29).

Bonus point (30).

ANSWER KEY FOR PLOT-CHECK QUIZ ON CHAPTERS 1 AND 2

1. Lennie
2. George
3. Candy
4. Curley
5. Slim
6. The boss
7. George
8. Lennie
9. Curley's wife
10. Curley's wife
11. "This ain't no good place."
12. To own a little farm
13. George
14. Lennie
15. Lennie
16. Tried to touch a girl's dress
17. Carlson
18. Crooks
19. George
20. Lennie
21. The bush by the river.
22. Lennie
23. George
24. Slim
25. Curley
26. Curley's wife
27. George
28. Curley

29–30. George protected Lennie. Curley was a bully who hated "big guys."

SCORE: $30 \times 2 = 60$

(30 minus number wrong = number right $\times 2 = x/60$)

PLOT-CHECK QUIZ ON *OF MICE AND MEN*: CHAPTERS 3 and 4

Directions: These answers may be used once, more than once, or not at all because some are false and not all answers have been included. Sometimes you must provide your own answers. Put answers on your own paper, *not* on this quiz.

♦ John Steinbeck	♦ George Milton	♦ Lennie Small	♦ Carlson
♦ Candy	♦ Curley	♦ Curley's wife	♦ The boss
♦ Slim	♦ Crooks	♦ Whit	♦ Clara
♦ Andy Cushman	♦ Heaven	♦ Money in the bank	♦ Having loyal friends

He (1) shot Candy's old, lame dog.

His (2) opinions were law because he was the (3).

He (4) had saved $350.00 that he wanted to use to buy into George and Lennie's dream.

He (5) was a young farm hand who wanted to know if his friend, Bill Tenner, has seen his letter to the editor in a pulp magazine.

This person (6) told this person (7), "I think you got your han' caught in a machine. If you don't tell nobody what happened, we ain't going to. But you jus' tell an' try to get this guy (8) canned and we'll tell ever'body, an' then will you get the laugh."

He (9) wanted to cook and do odd jobs on George and Lennie's farm without pay. He first told his wish to (10) when they were alone in the bunkhouse.

During the same conversation, he (11) told (12) that "A guy needs somebody—to be near him.... A guy goes nuts if he ain't got nobody. Don't make no difference who the guy is, long's he's with you.... I tell ya a guy gets too lonely an' he gets sick."

Curley's wife *did* believe that Curley's hand had been crushed in a machine because she saw it happen. (13) True or false. If false, explain.

This person (14) referred to this person (15) as a "machine."

His (16) eyes were described as being "God-like."

He (17) got into a fight with this person (18) because he thought he was being laughed at by him.

This person (19) told this person (20), "I could get you strung up on a tree so easy it ain't even funny."

He (21) compared owning your own land to (22).

According to him (23), "Nobody gets to heaven, and nobody gets no land. It's just in their head."

He (24) became angry and upset when he found out that he (25) had told some of the other men about their dream.

ANSWER KEY FOR PLOT-CHECK QUIZ ON CHAPTERS 3 AND 4

1. Carlson
2. Slim
3. Foreman
4. Candy
5. Whit
6. Slim
7. Curley
8. Lennie
9. Crooks
10. Lennie
11. Crooks
12. Lennie
13. False because he noticed marks on Lennie's face and called him a "machine."
14. Curley's wife
15. Lennie
16. Slim
17. Lennie
18. Curley
19. Curley's wife
20. Crooks
21. Crooks
22. Heaven
23. Crooks
24. George
25. Lennie

SCORE: 25 × 2 = 50

(25 minus number wrong = number right × 2 = $x/50$)

PLOT-CHECK QUIZ ON *OF MICE AND MEN*: CHAPTERS 5 AND 6

Directions: These answers may be used once, more than once, or not at all because some are false and not all answers have been included. Sometimes you must provide your own answers. Put answers on your own paper, *not* on this quiz.

- John Steinbeck
- George Milton
- Lennie Small
- Carlson
- Candy
- Curley
- Curley's wife
- The boss
- Slim
- Crooks
- Aunt Clara
- He killed a puppy.
- He had stolen rabbits
- He would never own his own farm.
- A giant rabbit
- Bush by the river
- Their dream farm
- Leave him
- Not fit to tend rabbits

He (1) worried that he (2) wouldn't let him tend the rabbits because (3).

He (4) was the first to discover the corpse of Curley's wife.

He (5) wanted to let Lennie escape after killing Curley's wife but he (6) wanted to have Lennie lynched. In fact, he wanted to shoot him himself.

After the death of Curley's wife, Candy's greatest fear was (7).

Before George found Lennie in (8), Lennie imagined that he heard the voices of (9) and (10).

By having Lennie hear voices at this point in the story, Steinbeck is implying that Lennie did have a (11).

After the death of Curley's wife, Lennie heard someone (12) speaking to him: "I tol' you an' tol' you. I tol' you, 'Min' George because he's such a nice fella an' good to you.' But you don't take no care. You do bad things."

Another voice (13) told Lennie that he was (14) and that he (15) "was gonna beat hell outa" him and then that he was going to (16).

The men in the bunk house thought that he (17) had taken Carlson's Luger but he (18) had really taken it.

George allowed the farm hands believe that he (19) had taken Carlson's Luger because George needed time to (20).

When Curley discovered that George had killed Lennie, he was very angry because he had wanted to do it himself. (21) True or false. If false, explain briefly.

When George finally found Lennie, he immediately "gave him hell" for "doing a bad thing." (22) True or false. If false, explain.

Lennie never did realize that George was going to kill him. (23) True or false. If false, explain.

Just before George killed Lennie, he talked about (24).

He (25) wanted him (26) to know that he had never been really angry with him for anything that he had done in the past.

He (27) alone assured George that he had done the right thing to kill Lennie.

The story concludes with this farm hand (28) asking another (29), "Now what the hell ya suppose is eatin' them two guys?"

George was arrested by the sheriff for the murder of Lennie. (30) True or false. If false, explain.

ANSWER KEY FOR PLOT-CHECK QUIZ ON CHAPTERS 5 AND 6

1. Lennie
2. George
3. he had killed a puppy.
4. Candy
5. Candy
6. Curley
7. the loss of their farm.
8. the bushes by the river
9. Aunt Clara
10. a giant rabbit
11. conscience or a sense of right and wrong.
12. Aunt Clara
13. a giant rabbit
14. not fit to tend rabbits
15. George
16. leave him.
17. Lennie
18. George
19. Lennie
20. plan what to do about Lennie.
21. False. Curley was in awe that Lennie was dead already.
22. False. George knew it was too late to berate Lennie about anything. He felt only pity.
23. True.
24. their dream of the farm.
25. George
26. Lennie
27. Slim
28. Carlson
29. Curley
30. False. The story ends with Slim trying to console George.

SCORE: $30 \times 2 = 60$
(30 minus number wrong = number right $\times 2 = x/60$)

TRIVIA QUIZ ON THE AMERICAN DREAM

1. Which company invites you to *eat* the American dream?
2. What company claims that it has been "*Protecting* the American dream for over fifty years"?
3. What is the "American dream *car*"?
4. What newspaper says that it is "*The daily diary* of the American dream"?
5. Which NFL team as made a video entitled, "Living the American Dream"?
6. Which Chicago newspaper claims that it is "The official sponsor of American dreams"?
7. According to this group of people, "Where does the American dream begin"?
8. According to Lionel Trilling, what is "The only nation in the world that prides itself upon a dream and gives its name to one"?
9. What former coach of the Chicago Bears claims that he *is* the American dream?
10. Which state license plate proclaims that it is "The land of opportunity"?

ANSWER KEY

1. Edy's "American Dream" ice cream (vanilla).
2. Olympia Paints.
3. Cadillac
4. The Wall Street Journal
5. The Dallas Cowboys
6. The Chicago Sun-Times
7. The National Education Association
8. America (of course!)
9. Mike "Da Bears" Ditka
10. Arkansas

WHAT IS THE AMERICAN DREAM?—A DEFINITION

The American dream is:

- A *belief* in the
- Unlimited *progress* of all our citizens (who have been created equal, and endowed by their Creator with the rights to life, liberty, and the pursuit of happiness)
- Towards a goal of complete *happiness* (independence, individuality, wealth, success, power, fame, freedom, etc.)
- Which was once attained in the *past*
- And which is attainable again in the *future*
- (If we make the effort),
- Here on the Earth,
- In this Land, America!

DEFINITIONS OF THE AMERICAN DREAM

- "We hold these truths to be self-evident, that all men are created equal, that they are endowed by their Creator with certain unalienable rights, that among these are life, liberty, and *the pursuit of happiness*. That to secure these rights governments are instituted among men...that whenever any form of government becomes destructive of these ends, it is the right of the people to alter or to abolish it."—Thomas Jefferson
- The phrase was first coined by James Truslow Adams in his *Epic of America* (1931): The American dream is "that dream of a better, richer, and happier life for all our citizens of every rank which is *the greatest contribution we have as yet made to the thought and welfare of the world*" (Preface, viii).
- The American dream "was *rebirth*, the eternal, haunting craving of men to be born again, the yearning for the second chance. The New World was that chance...its coat of arms bore and bears only one word—*Freedom*...the condition in which a man feels like a human being, like himself. It is the purpose, the definition, and consequence of rebirth. It is the Dream."— Eric Sevareid
- Essentially, the American dream is as old as the mind of man; we find it always in some country of the Western world. The Garden of Eden, Atlantis, Utopia, Brook Farm, and so forth.
- The discovery of the New World, the New Canaan (to the Puritans and Pilgrims), gave reality to the old myth and suggested the possible realization of it on earth, that is, in this New Land, America.
- "Ours is the only nation that prides itself upon a dream and gives its name to one—the American dream."—Lionel Trilling
- Each generation, and nearly every author of American literature, accepts the challenge to answer the basic question posed by the dream: "Is the American dream only a dream or is it a goal worth pursuing?"—Frederic Carpenter

BASIC QUESTIONS FOR *OF MICE AND MEN*

BASIC QUESTION NO. 1

According to Steinbeck, is the American dream an illusion that people foolishly pursue?
If *yes*, then:

1. Why does Steinbeck have George describe his and Lennie's dream in realistic, attainable terms? (pp. 16, 62)
2. Why does Steinbeck have Candy's money make George's and Lennie's dream a real possibility? (pp.65, 84)
3. Why does Steinbeck have the skeptic Crooks momentarily want to become part of George and Lennie's dream? (p. 84)
4. Why isn't George angry when he discovers that Lennie's accidental killing of Curley's wife means that they will never realize their dream? (pp. 104, 116-17)
5. Why does Steinbeck have owning their own farm mean independence for George and Candy? (pp. 63, 66)

If *no*, then:

6. Does Steinbeck have George and Lennie fail to achieve their dream because George never really believe in it? (p. 116)
7. Why does Steinbeck have Curley's wife fail to get to Hollywood? (p. 96)
8. Are we to conclude that George's and Lennie's failure to reach their dream was merely "something that happened"? (Original title of the novel)
9. Why *do* the "best made plans of mice and men (sometimes) go astray? (Actual title of the novel and an allusion to Robert Burn's poem)
10. Does Steinbeck want us to believe that George relies too much on Lennie remembering what to do? (pp. 4, 17, 32, 60, 79, 81)

BASIC QUESTION NO. 2

Why does Steinbeck have George and Lennie fail to achieve their idea of the American dream? Rephrased: According to the story, why do the best made plans of mice and men (George and Lennie) sometimes go wrong?

1. Does Steinbeck want us to think that George depends too much on Lennie to do what he tells him to do? (pp. 32, 33, 60, 91)
2. Early in the story, why does George ignore Lennie's plea to "get outta here" because it was a "mean" place? (p. 36)
3. Why does Steinbeck emphasize that Lennie has trouble remembering things? (pp. 4, 17, 79)
4. Why does George go into town knowing that Lennie could get into trouble when he was away? (p. 78)
5. Why doesn't George seem to realize that Lennie doesn't know the extent of his enormous strength?
6. Why does Steinbeck have the need for companionship lead to the destruction of Curley's wife and, as a result, to the destruction of Lennie? (p. 99)
7. Why is George angry when he finds out that Lennie had told Candy and Crooks about their dream? (p. 91)
8. Why does Steinbeck have Crooks momentarily believe in George's and Lennie's dream but then have him bitterly denounce it? (p. 84)
9. Why does Steinbeck have Candy want to buy into George's and Lennie's dream? (pp. 65, 84)
10. After Curley's wife is dead, why does George think he has to kill Lennie? (p. 104)
11. Why does George finally admit that he knew "from the first" that he and Lennie would never achieve their dream? (p. 103)
12. Why isn't George angry when he discovers that Lennie's killing of Candy's wife means the end of their dream? (pp. 104, 116–117)

LESSON PLAN 6: *THE LITTLE PRINCE*

1. Focus:	Who was the most interesting child that you have ever met? What was unique or special about him or her? (5 minutes)
2. Objective:	To solve several questions of interpretation about the overall meaning of the novel.
3. Purpose:	To increase our mutual understanding (comprehension) and, as a result, our enjoyment of the story. To develop the habit of independent and critical thinking.
4. Input:	Begin with a factual quiz to check that everyone has read the novel. (Rule 1: No one may participate who has not read the selection.) The quiz should be ten factual questions, short answers (not True/False). Those with 70% are in the inner circle; those with less are in the outer circle. (15 minutes) Two or four basic questions. Handout follows. (30 or 60 minutes)
5. Modeling, checking, and guided practice:	During discussion the co-leaders model the four rules of discussion, and check for understanding by asking follow-up questions for clarification, substantiation, consistency, relevance, implication, resolution, and to get more opinion. Guided practice is the discussion.
6. Closure:	Oral or written resolution of one or two basic questions just discussed. What was so memorable about the little prince for the narrator? For you?

During Socratic Seminar day(s), in a full 90-minute period, four pairs of student co-leaders each lead a 15-minute discussion of the reading. It is important that the teacher approves the student co-leaders' questions before discussion to avoid wasting time on questions that are not clear, are factual, or evaluative. (Discussion should center on solving problems, not on trying to figure out what the problems are.) During the remaining time (if any) the teacher leads a demonstration discussion (modeling) of one of his or her basic questions on the reading of the lesson.

TEXT: St. Exupery, A. (1943). *The Little Prince.* New York: Harbrace Paperbound Library.

BASIC QUESTION FOR *THE LITTLE PRINCE*

Why does the author believe that children understand life better than adults?

1. According to the little prince, why do grown-ups never understand anything by themselves? (p. 4)
2. Why does it irritate the little prince that grown-ups "always need to have things explained"? (p. 4)
3. Why did the narrator, a marooned pilot, mention that grown-ups encouraged him to give up drawing and get into geography, history, math, or grammar? (pp. 4, 6)
4. Why hasn't living so long among grown-ups improved the narrator's opinion of them? (p. 5)
5. Unlike children who are concerned with "essential matters," why do grown-ups love "matters of consequence" and numbers? (pp. 5, 16, 28, 56–57)
6. Why does the narrator believe that children must show great forbearance towards grown-ups? (p. 17)
7. According to the narrator, are "those who understand life" only children? (pp. 17, 89, 94)
8. After meeting *the king*, why does the little prince conclude that "grown-ups are very strange"? (p. 47)
9. Why can't the little prince understand why *the conceited man* wants to be admired so much? (p. 50)
10. Why does the little prince feel sorry for *the alcoholic?* (p. 50)
11. Why does the little prince dismiss *the business man's* claim to own stars as a matter of "no great consequence"? (p. 56)
12. Why had the little prince earlier referred to the business man as a mushroom? (p. 29)
13. Why is *the lamplighter* the only grown-up that the little prince would have wanted to befriend? (pp. 57–62)
14. Why does *the old geographer* impress the little prince as someone with "a real profession" when he does not explore the world but only record the discoveries of others? (pp. 62–66)
15. Unlike some adults, once the little prince asks a question, why does he never let go of it? (p. 66)

16. Why does the little prince get angry when the pilot narrator tries to repair his aircraft? (p. 28)
17. Why does the little prince never answer questions? (pp. 92, 98, 113)
18. Why does the author have little prince meet a railway switcher who keeps moving people about who do not know where they are going? (p. 89)
19. Why does the little prince tell the merchant that he would rather drink water than take a pill? (p. 89)
20. Why does the little prince say that "only children [not men] know what they are looking for? (pp. 89, 94)
21. According to the narrator, why will no grown-up ever understand the importance of the question about whether or not a sheep has eaten the little prince's rose? (p. 111)

SOME ALTERNATIVE BASIC QUESTIONS

Here are three more basic questions that you can qualify for discussion if you can come up with at least eight related interpretive follow-up questions for each. When students are struggling to write their own basic questions, I sometimes give them a basic question as an intermediate step to writing their own clusters. They then have to develop at least eight of their own related interpretive follow-up questions.

BASIC QUESTION NO. 2

What does the pilot narrator want most to remember about his friend the little prince?

BASIC QUESTION NO. 3

Of the six planets that the little prince visits, why is each inhabited by only one person?

BASIC QUESTION NO. 4

Does St. Exupery suggest that the little prince is the Christ child returned to earth?

CAVEAT

The model basic questions that accompany the Lesson Plan for each reading are *not* intended to be ready-made questions that you can try out on a group. The issues they raise, the questions they pose, are meant to make you think harder and better about *your own* questions. To be sure, next to asking good spontaneous follow-up questions, the hardest part of the Socratic method is coming up with your own questions about the readings. Why? There are no answer keys for discussion and because thinking is difficult! Nevertheless, the rewards are great.

LESSON PLAN 7: *RUNNING LOOSE*

1. Focus:	What is your biggest problem in high school? (5 minutes)
2. Objective:	To solve several questions of interpretation about the overall meaning of the novel.
3. Purpose:	To increase our mutual understanding (comprehension) and, as a result, our enjoyment of the story. To develop the habit of independent and critical thinking.
4. Input:	Begin with a factual quiz to check that everyone has read the novel. (Rule 1: No one may participate who has not read the selection.) The quiz should be ten factual questions, short answers (not True/False). Those with 70% are in the inner circle; those with less are in the outer circle. (15 minutes) Two or four basic questions. Handout follows. (30 or 60 minutes)
5. Modeling, checking, and guided practice:	During discussion the co-leaders model the four rules of discussion, and check for understanding by asking follow-up questions for clarification, substantiation, consistency, relevance, implication, resolution, and to get more opinion. Guided practice is the discussion.
6. Closure:	Oral or written resolution of one or two basic questions just discussed. Or complete the Exercise on Textual Analysis. Handout follows.

During Socratic Seminar day(s), in a full 90-minute period, four pairs of student co-leaders each lead a 15-minute discussion of the reading. It is important that the teacher approves the student co-leaders' questions before discussion to avoid wasting time on questions that are not clear, are factual, or evaluative. (Discussion should center on solving problems, not on trying to figure out what the problems are.) During the remaining time (if any) the teacher leads a demonstration discussion (modeling) of one of his or her basic questions on the reading of the lesson.

TEXT: Crutcher, C. (1983). *Running Loose.* New York: Bantam Doubleday Dell Books.

BASIC QUESTIONS FOR *RUNNING LOOSE*

BASIC QUESTION NO. 1

Why does Louie quit the team to protest the coach's order to play dirty?

1. Which of Louie's character traits revealed in the first chapter (pp. 9–15) are related to his quitting the football team?
2. What is the difference between the advice that Dakota and Norm give Louie when he needs help with a problem? (pp. 21, 25, 37, 68, 80, 89, 138–141, 145–147)
3. When Boomer disables Washington, why does Louie quit the team immediately rather than wait until the game was over? (p. 1)
4. Why does Becky advise Louie not to make a cause out of the coach's order to play dirty football? (pp. 70–72)
5. Does Louie accept Carter's explanation for not joining his protest? (p. 78)
6. Why do both Jasper and Arney complain about Louie's "language" when Washington was hurt? (pp. 62, 82)
7. Why does the author use Jasper's phrase "running loose" as the story's title? (pp. 95, 185)
8. What "special connection" does Louie feel with Washington? (p. 102)
9. Why does coach Madison encourage Louie to join the track team?
10. When Louie agrees to Jasper's conditions for joining the track team, what does he mean when he says "you got to take care of yourself"? (p. 162)
11. According to Louie, why is there no use in being honorable with dishonorable men? (p. 189)
12. Why does Louie think he should have learned to like people who don't like him? (p. 190)

BASIC QUESTION NO. 2

Why does Louie have such a difficult time dealing with Becky's death?

1. What does Louie want to remember that Becky said about sex? (p. 117)

2. What does Becky mean that you don't have to have sex to make love? (p. 118)
3. Why is Louie glad he did *not* have sex with Becky? (p. 118)
4. Why does Louie again refer to his theory of relationships just before he relates the details of Becky's fatal accident? (p. 121)
5. Why does Louie think God owes him an explanation for Becky's death? (p. 126)
6. Why does Louie refer to God an the "Old Geezer"? (p. 129)
7. What kind of deal did Louie try to make with God during Becky's funeral? (p. 135)
8. Why does Louie get so angry about ministers who make excuses for all the rotten things that happen in life? (p. 137)
9. What does Dakota mean when he tells Louie "you get no place" blaming God? (p. 139)
10. What is the point of Dakota's rule-less game of checkers? (p. 141)

SOME ALTERNATIVE QUESTIONS

Here is a list of alternative interpretive questions that should help you to think about your own questions that you would like to bring up in discussion when you are a co-leader.

1. In the first chapter, what important character traits does the author have his narrator (Louie Banks) reveal about himself? (pp. 9–15)
2. Which of Louie's character traits does the author regard as the most important?
3. What does Louie mean by "getting your act down"? (pp. 15, 23)
4. What does Louie admire about Carter? (pp. 15, 23, 170–171)
5. Why does Louie refer to his mother and father by their first names?
6. What is Louie's "theory" about " guys and girls and love affairs"? (pp. 16–17)
7. Early in the story, why does Louie say he could not have gotten through his senior year without his parents? (p. 27)
8. Why does Carter tell Boomer that if they played to hurt Washington it would mean that they think he is better than them? (p. 59)

9. Why does Carter admit to Louie that he did not quit the team because he did not want to throw away his chance at a scholarship? (p. 78)
10. Why is it likely that Jasper knew Lednecky lied when he said he did not order his players to play dirty football? (pp. 84, 179)
11. When he spoke of his meeting with Jasper regarding Louie's suspension, what does Norm mean by "these kinds of negotiations." (p. 97)
12. Why is Norm willing to lie to Brenda about Louie staying over night with Becky? (pp. 111, 112)
13. What is the point of Dakota's question about getting hit by a truck? (p. 141)
14. Does coach Madison encourage Louie to join the track team to help him get over Becky's loss or because he wants a confrontation with coach Lednecky? (p. 151)
15. What does Madison mean when he tells Lednecky "We can *show* them [players] ways to live their lives, but we can't *tell* them"? (p. 156)
16. Why does Madison lie when Jasper asks if he had anything to do with the phone call from Fred Sanders? (p. 162)
17. Why does Louie lie repeatedly (four times) to Jasper about destroying Becky's memorial plaque? (pp. 178–180)
18. When Louie competes against Washington in the two-mile race, why does he recall his previous mile race against Boomer? (pp. 34–35, 182)
19. Why does Louie answer truthfully Jasper's questions about why someone would have been offended by what was on Becky's plaque? (p. 188)
20. Why does Louie think Jasper understood his objections to Becky's plaque? (p. 189)
21. Why does the novel end with Louie planning to destroy the new plaque that Jasper put on Becky's memorial tree? (p. 190)

CAVEAT

The model basic questions that accompany the Lesson Plan for each reading are *not* intended to be ready-made questions that you can try out on a group.

The issues they raise, the questions they pose, are meant to make you think harder and better about *your own* questions. To be sure, next to asking good spontaneous follow-up questions, the hardest part of the Socratic method is coming up with your own questions about the readings. Why? There are no answer keys for discussion and because thinking is difficult! Nevertheless, the rewards are great.

EXERCISE ON TEXTUAL ANALYSIS OF *RUNNING LOOSE*

(Review pages 16–17)

Technique: Go over the following passage (pp. 189–190) line-by-line, freely asking any question of fact or interpretation that it raises in your mind—either about these lines or about anything else in the novel that comes to mind. This is a particularly good passage for textual analysis because it somewhat sums up what Louie has gotten from his senior year of high school.

> I learned a lot this year, in spite of the fact that I was going to school. I learned something about friendship and a whole lot about love and that there's no use being honorable with dishonorable men. There's nothing they can do to you when you don't care anymore. I learned to accept myself even though I'm not Clint Eastwood or Joe Montana or Carter Sampson, and that you can get through almost anything if you have people around you who care about you. And I learned that when all is said and done, you're responsible for every damn thing you do. Most important, I learned how jacked up you can get just being alive and what a vicious, miserable, ugly thing death is. I'm going to stay away from it if I can.
>
> A few things I didn't learn. I didn't learn to like people who don't like me, and I didn't learn not to push my luck. About a week and a half ago they set a new plaque in concrete beside Becky's tree. Jasper didn't take my advice; it was a duplicate of the other one. What Jasper did do was camp out overnight in his office for about a week with a .22 loaded with bird shot, waiting for me to show. But I've learned patience. He's tucked away at home in his own bed tonight, visions of beating me to death with a blunt instrument dancing in his head. In about five minutes I'm going down to the station to get the hammer.

LESSON PLAN 8: *OUT OF THE SILENT PLANET*

1. Focus:	Do you believe that there is rational life on other planets? If yes, could that rational life be a different species than our own (homo sapiens)?
2. Objective:	To solve several questions of interpretation about the overall meaning of the novel.
3. Purpose:	To increase our mutual understanding (comprehension) and, as a result, our enjoyment of the story. To develop the habit of independent and critical thinking.
4. Input:	Begin with a factual quiz to check that everyone has read the novel. (Rule 1: No one may participate who has not read the selection.) The quiz should be ten factual questions, short answers (not True/False). Those with 70% are in the inner circle; those with less are in the outer circle. (15 minutes) Two to four basic questions. Handout follows. (30 or 60 minutes)
5. Modeling, checking, and guided practice:	During discussion the co-leaders model the four rules of discussion, and check for understanding by asking follow-up questions for clarification, substantiation, consistency, relevance, implication, resolution, and to get more opinion. Guided practice is the discussion.
6. Closure:	Oral or written resolution of one or two basic questions just discussed. Will space travel become exploitation or adventure?

During Socratic Seminar day(s), in a full 90-minute period, four pairs of student co-leaders each lead a 15-minute discussion of the reading. It is important that the teacher approves the student co-leaders' questions before discussion to avoid wasting time on questions that are not clear, are factual, or evaluative. (Discussion should center on solving problems, not on trying to figure out what the problems are.) During the remaining time (if any) the teacher leads a demonstration discussion (modeling) of one of his or her basic questions on the reading of the lesson.

TEXT: Lewis, C.S. (1996). *Out of the Silent Planet*. New York: Scribners.

BASIC QUESTION FOR *OUT OF THE SILENT PLANET*

Why does the author contrast the greed and arrogance of Devine and Weston with the sensitivity and intelligence of Ransom?

1. Why does Ransom volunteer to get Harry back from Devine and Watson? (p. 9)
2. When Ransom first encounters Devine and Watson, why does he feel as though he had "blundered on something criminal"? (p. 13)
3. Unlike Weston, why doesn't Devine care about the future of mankind? (p. 30)
4. Unlike Devine and Watson, why is Ransom so awed by the beauty of Malacandra? (p. 42)
5. Why does the narrator want us to know that Devine's sole interest in space travel is "the sun's blood" (gold)? (p. 69)
6. Why does Ransom tell Oyarsa that he would sacrifice himself to prevent Devine and Watson from exploiting Malacandra? (p. 123)
7. Why does Weston think that he can intimidate Oyarsa and the people? (p. 128)
8. Why does Ransom have a religious experience during the funeral of the three *knau*? (p. 131)
9. When Devine sees the cremation of *hrossa,* why does Devine think only of its use for covering up a murder? (p. 132)
10. Why does Weston believe that he may wipe out the Malacandrians because of "the right of the higher over the lower"? (p. 135)
11. What does Weston mean when he tells Oyarsa that "Life is greater than any system of morality"? (p. 136)
12. Why does Weston care only for Man and his race? (p. 138)
13. Why is Devine described as "broken" and Watson as "bent"? (p. 139)
14. When asked why he came to Malacandra, why does Weston reply to "Make man live all the time" (p. 139)

SOME ALTERNATIVE BASIC QUESTIONS

Here are three more basic questions that you can qualify for discussion if you can come up with at least eight related interpretive follow-up questions for each. When students are struggling to write their own basic questions, I sometimes give them a basic question as an intermediate step to writing their own clusters. They then have to develop at least eight of their own related interpretive follow-up questions.

BASIC QUESTION NO. 2

Although Malacandra is primitive and dying, why does Lewis portray it as superior to Earth's civilization?

BASIC QUESTION NO. 3

Why do the Malacandrians believe in one god, Maleldil?

BASIC QUESTION NO. 4

Why does Ransom return from Malacandra even though he knows Earth's future is so bleak?

CAVEAT

The model basic questions that accompany the Lesson Plan for each reading are *not* intended to be ready-made questions that you can try out on a group. The issues they raise, the questions they pose, are meant to make you think harder and better about *your own* questions. To be sure, next to asking good spontaneous follow-up questions, the hardest part of the Socratic method is coming up with your own questions about the readings. Why? There are no answer keys for discussion and because thinking is difficult! Nevertheless, the rewards are great.

LESSON PLAN 9: *THE LIGHT IN THE FOREST*

1. Focus:	What would you do if you were told today that you were not (Tom Smith) but John Butler? (5 minutes)
2. Objective:	To solve several questions of interpretation about the overall meaning of the novel.
3. Purpose:	To increase our mutual understanding (comprehension) and, as a result, our enjoyment of the story. To develop the habit of independent and critical thinking.
4. Input:	Begin with a factual quiz to check that everyone has read the novel. (Rule 1: No one may participate who has not read the selection.) The quiz should be ten factual questions, short answers (not True/False). Those with 70% are in the inner circle; those with less are in the outer circle. (15 minutes)
	Two or four basic questions. Handouts follow. (30 or 60 minutes)
5. Modeling, checking, and guided practice:	During discussion the co-leaders model the four rules of discussion, and check for understanding by asking follow-up questions for clarification, substantiation, consistency, relevance, implication, resolution, and to get more opinion. Guided practice is the discussion.
6. Closure:	Oral or written resolution of one or two basic questions just discussed.

During Socratic Seminar day(s), in a full 90-minute period, four pairs of student co-leaders each lead a 15-minute discussion of the reading. It is important that the teacher approves the student co-leaders' questions before discussion to avoid wasting time on questions that are not clear, are factual, or evaluative. (Discussion should center on solving problems, not on trying to figure out what the problems are.) During the remaining time (if any) the teacher leads a demonstration discussion (modeling) of one of his or her basic questions on the reading of the lesson.

TEXT: Richter, C. (1953). *The Light in the Forest.* New York: Ballantine, Fawcett Juniper Books.

BASIC QUESTION FOR *THE LIGHT IN THE FOREST*

By betraying his own brothers in warning the whites of an ambush, how did True Son remain true of himself?

1. Why does the narrator never refer to the boy as John Butler but only as "True Son"?
2. Why is leaving Gordie the only thing that True Son regrets when he runs away from his white family? (p. 88)
3. Why does the sight of a child's scalp upset True Son so much? (pp. 64, 108)
4. Why doesn't True Son reflect more on whether or not he wanted to act as a decoy? (p. 109)
5. Why does the author have True Son dream about his white family just before the ambush? (p. 109)
6. Why does True Son want to see if he is the white child in his dream? (p. 109)
7. Why does the sight of a boy who is Gordie's age trigger True Son's betrayal of his brothers? (p. 112)
8. Why didn't True Son himself understand his betrayal of his brothers? (p. 114)
9. Why does True Son never feel more like an Indian than during his trial? (p. 115)
10. Does True Son understand why Cuyloga at first defends him but then finally rejects him? (pp. 116–118)
11. How can True Son have the heart and the head of a true Indian but not his blood? (p. 118)
12. Why does True Son never love his father more than when he stands to defend and reject him during the trial? (p. 118)
13. When Cuyloga rejects him, why does True Son ask in despair, "Who *is* my father"? (p. 119)
14. Why does the author have True Son prefer the first living death to the second? (p. 119)

SOME ALTERNATIVE BASIC QUESTIONS

Here are three more basic questions that you can qualify for discussion if you can come up with at least eight related interpretive follow-up questions for each. When students are struggling to write their own basic questions, I sometimes give them a basic question as an intermediate step to writing their own clusters. They then have to develop at least eight of their own related interpretive follow-up questions.

BASIC QUESTION NO. 2

Why are the Indians and the white's unable to understand one another's cultural values?

BASIC QUESTION NO. 3

In his portrayal of the White and Indian cultures, has the author been fair to them both, as he claims in his Acknowledgments?

BASIC QUESTION NO. 4

Why does Conrad Richter believe that by understanding the aversion of the First Americans for whites, Americans today would better understand the aversion of some African, European, and Asian peoples today?

CAVEAT

The model basic questions that accompany the Lesson Plan for each reading are *not* intended to be ready-made questions that you can try out on a group. The issues they raise, the questions they pose, are meant to make you think harder and better about *your own* questions. To be sure, next to asking good spontaneous follow-up questions, the hardest part of the Socratic method is coming up with your own questions about the readings. Why? There are no answer keys for discussion and because thinking is difficult! Nevertheless, the rewards are great.

LESSON PLAN 10: *THE TIME MACHINE*

1. Focus:	Journal writing: What does the poem by Robert Frost, *Fire and Ice,* have to do with the story of H.G. Wells? You can download this poem from the Internet at: http://www.bartleby.com/cgi-bin/texis/webinator/sitesearch
2. Objective:	To solve several questions of interpretation about the overall meaning of the novel.
3. Purpose:	To increase our mutual understanding (comprehension) and, as a result, our enjoyment of the story. To develop the habit of independent and critical thinking.
4. Input:	Begin with a factual quiz to check that everyone has read the novel. (Rule 1: No one may participate who has not read the selection.) The quiz should be ten factual questions, short answers (not True/False). Those with 70% are in the inner circle; those with less are in the outer circle. (15 minutes) Two or four basic questions. Handout follows. (30 or 60 minutes)
5. Modeling, checking, and guided practice:	During discussion the co-leaders model the four rules of discussion, and check for understanding by asking follow-up questions for clarification, substantiation, consistency, relevance, implication, resolution, and to get more opinion. Guided practice is the discussion.
6. Closure:	Oral or written resolution of one or two basic questions just discussed. and/or a discussion of the journal responses to the question about the poem *Fire and Ice.*

During Socratic Seminar day(s), in a full 90-minute period, four pairs of student co-leaders each lead a 15-minute discussion of the reading. It is important that the teacher approves the student co-leaders' questions before discussion to avoid wasting time on questions that are not clear, are factual, or evaluative. (Discussion should center on solving problems, not on trying to figure out what the problems are.) During the remaining time (if any) the teacher leads a demonstration discussion (modeling) of one of his or her basic questions on the reading of the lesson.

TEXT: Wells, H.G. (1968). *The Time Machine.* New York: Bantam Books.

BASIC QUESTION FOR *THE TIME MACHINE*

Does Wells want us to conclude that the betterment of mankind is doomed to failure?

If *yes*, then:

1. Why does the Time Traveler describe the Golden Age as one in which "the ideal of preventive medicine was attained"? (p. 38)
2. Why does the Time Traveler also see the Golden Age as an ecological paradise wherein man has achieved perfect comfort and security? (pp. 38, 49)
3. Why is the Time Traveler so impressed with the architectural achievements of the Golden Age? (p. 26)
4. Why does Wells have the Time Traveler note that among the Eloi there was no violence but "a social paradise" in which the ideal of Communism had been achieved? (pp. 38, 70, 71)
5. Why does Wells have the Time Traveler carry on a "miniature flirtation" with Weena? (pp. 53, 65, 70)
6. Why does Wells have his narrator note in the epilogue that "gratitude and mutual tenderness still lived on in the heart of man"? (p. 115)
7. Why does Wells conclude his story by having his narrator remain optimistic about mankind's future? (p. 114)
8. Why does Wells have both the Time Traveler and the narrator be so deeply moved by Weena's humanity?

If *no*, then:

9. Why does Wells have so many of the Time Traveler's theories about the Golden Age turn out to be wrong? (pp. 35, 40, 50, 60, 61)
10. Is Wells warning us that plans to perfect mankind are dangerous or that evolution will inevitably lead to man's degeneration?
11. Is Wells implying that attaining perfect harmony will destroy human intelligence? (p. 84, 97)
12. Why does Wells have Man evolve into two distinct species? (p. 58)
13. Unlike the Time Traveler, why are the Eloi unable to cope with the Morlocks? (pp. 72, 87)

14. Why is the Time Traveler more pessimistic than the narrator about mankind's future?
15. Why does Wells have the Time Traveler note that none among the Eloi made any effort to save Weena from drowning? (p. 52)
16. Does Wells agree that the triumph of technology and social organization will destroy humanity and freedom or is this view but another part of the Time Traveler's mistaken predictions about the future?

SOME ALTERNATIVE BASIC QUESTIONS

Here are three more basic questions that you can qualify for discussion if you can come up with at least eight related interpretive follow-up questions for each. When students are struggling to write their own basic questions, I sometimes give them a basic question as an intermediate step to writing their own clusters. They then have to develop at least eight of their own related interpretive follow-up questions.

BASIC QUESTION NO. 2

Why is Wells ambivalent (optimistic as well as pessimistic) about mankind's future?

BASIC QUESTION NO. 3

According to Wells, does technology expand or limit human freedom?

BASIC QUESTION NO. 4

According to Wells, can mankind have the benefits of technological progress without sacrificing its freedom and without becoming socially insensitive (mechanical and inhumane)?

CAVEAT

The model basic questions that accompany the Lesson Plan for each reading are *not* intended to be ready-made questions that you can try out on a group. The issues they raise, the questions they pose, are meant to make you think harder and better about *your own* questions. To be sure, next to asking good spontaneous follow-up questions, the hardest part of the Socratic method is coming up with your own questions about the readings. Why? There are no answer keys for discussion and because thinking is difficult! Nevertheless, the rewards are great.

PLOT-CHECK QUIZ FOR *THE TIME MACHINE*

Directions: Answer each question briefly in complete sentences in the space beneath it.

CHAPTER 1

1. What does the Time Traveler mean by the Fourth Dimension?
2. How did the Time Traveler demonstrate to his friends his intention to travel in time?

CHAPTER 2

3. What dramatic news does the Time Traveler have for his dinner guests when he arrives late?

CHAPTER 3

4. How does Wells remind the reader that the Time Traveler does not travel in space but in time?

CHAPTER 4

5. How do the creatures of 802,701 first react when they encounter the Time Traveler?
6. What two things struck the Time Traveler when he first encountered human life in 802,701?
7. What is the diet of the Eloi?
8. Why does there appear to be no differences among the sexes of the Eloi?
9. What is one of the apparent wonders of "the Golden Age" for the Time Traveler?

CHAPTER 5

10. What does the Time Traveler believe had happened to his Time Machine?

11. How does the Time Traveler make such a devoted friend among the Eloi?

12. Why does the Time Traveler think that mankind evolved into two distinct species?

CHAPTER 6

13. In what two important ways do the Morlocks differ from the Eloi?

CHAPTER 7

14. When the Time Traveler interrupts his story at this point, what does he put on the table before his guests?

15. What horrific conclusion does the Time Traveler suddenly make about the diet of the Morlocks?

CHAPTER 8

16. What was the Palace of Green Porcelain?

17. Why does the Time Traveler want to visit the Palace of Green Porcelain?

CHAPTER 9

18. When the Time Traveler builds a fire to hold off the Morlocks, why was it a terrible mistake?

19. What drove the Morlocks into a frenzy when they surrounded the Time Traveler?

20. When the Morlocks went into a frenzy and he could not find Weena, what did the Time Traveler ask God to do?

21. When the Time Traveler returned to the white sphinx to find his Time Machine, why was he so sad?

CHAPTER 10

22. Where does the Time Traveler find his Time Machine?

23. Why does the plan of the Morlocks to trap the Time Traveler fail?

CHAPTER 11

24. When the Time Traveler inadvertently thrusts his machine forward, how far into the future does he travel?

25. What does the Time Traveler find in the distant future?

26. Why does this vision of the distant future so disturb the Time Traveler?

CHAPTER 12

27. After the Time Traveler's return to the present, how do his guests react to his account of the future?

28. How did the Time Traveler reassure himself that he *had* indeed traveled in time?

29. When the Time Traveler again travels in time, what kind of proof does he plan to return with to the present?

30. In the Epilogue, what are the feelings of the narrator when he reflects on the future of mankind?

FILM VERSION

See page 53 for guidleines to conduct a comparison-contrast discussion of the film version of the novel.

LESSON PLAN 11: *A GAME OF CATCH*

1. Focus:	Journal writing: In what ways is daily living like a game of catch? (10 minutes)
2. Objective:	To solve several questions of interpretation about the overall meaning of the story.
3. Purpose:	To increase our mutual understanding (comprehension) and, as a result, our enjoyment of the story. To develop the habit of independent and critical thinking.
4. Input:	Begin with a factual quiz to check that everyone has read the novel. Handout follows. (Rule 1: No one may participate who has not read the selection.) The quiz should be ten factual questions, short answers (not True/False). Those with 70% are in the inner circle; those with less are in the outer circle. (15 minutes) Three basic questions. Handout follows. (30 or 60 minutes)
5. Modeling, checking, and guided practice:	During discussion the co-leaders model the four rules of discussion, and check for understanding by asking follow-up questions for clarification, substantiation, consistency, relevance, implication, resolution, and to get more opinion. Guided practice is the discussion.
6. Closure:	Oral or written resolution of one or two basic questions just discussed.

PLOT-CHECK QUIZ FOR *A GAME OF CATCH*

Directions: First, answer each question briefly in a complete sentence in the space beneath it. Second, label the kind of question by marking at the left *Fact* for factual, *Int* for interpretation, and *Eval* for evaluation.

_____ 1. Why does Scho keep playing his game even after he falls from the tree?

_____ 2. Did Glennie or Monk make more of an effort to include Scho in their game of catch?

_____ 3. How did Glennie and Monk force Scho out of their game of catch?

_____ 4. If you were Glennie, how would you have told Scho that you didn't want to play with him without hurting his feelings?

_____ 5. Does the author want us to believe that Glennie and Monk treat Scho unfairly?

_____ 6. Have you ever felt treated unfairly when playing a game?

_____ 7. Why didn't Scho come down from the tree when Glennie asked him to play catch?

_____ 8. What title would you have given this story?

_____ 9. How did Scho feel when he said his last words?

_____ 10. Why did Scho pretend that he could control the actions of Glennie and Monk?

ANSWER KEY

Factual (2, 3, and 9); Interpretation (1, 5, 7, and 10); Evaluation (4, 6, and 8)

BASIC QUESTION FOR *A GAME OF CATCH*

Why does Scho pretend that he can control Monk and Glennie's actions?

ALTERNATIVE BASIC QUESTIONS

Here are two more basic questions that you can qualify for discussion if you can come up with at least eight related interpretive follow-up questions for each. When students are struggling to write their own basic questions, I sometimes give them a basic question as an intermediate step to writing their own clusters. They then have to develop at least eight of their own related interpretive follow-up questions.

BASIC QUESTION NO. 2

Does the author want us to believe that Glennie and Monk treated Scho unfairly?

BASIC QUESTION NO. 3

Why does Scho keep playing his game even after he fell from the tree?

CAVEAT

The model basic questions that accompany the Lesson Plan for each reading are *not* intended to be ready-made questions that you can try out on a group. The issues they raise, the questions they pose, are meant to make you think harder and better about *your own* questions. To be sure, next to asking good spontaneous follow-up questions, the hardest part of the Socratic method is coming up with your own questions about the readings. Why? There are no answer keys for discussion and because thinking is difficult! Nevertheless, the rewards are great.

LESSON PLAN 12: *TWO SOLDIERS*

Lesson 1:	Factual quiz on the story (pp. 150–152). While viewing film version of the story, list ten important differences between the two.
Lesson 2:	Write your own resolution to the story and then compare yours with five student models Exercises 1 and 2. Handout follows.
Lesson 3:	Write an essay on why Faulkner would not have approved the film's resolution to his story Exercise 4. Handout follows.

1. Focus:	Should movie producers and directors remain faithful to an author's original story? If so, why so? If not, why not?
2. Objective:	To understand how changing the plot changes the meaning (theme) of a story.
3. Purpose:	To understand why Faulkner would not have approved of the resolution in the movie version. (It changes his theme.)
4. Input:	Begin with a plot-check quiz Handout follows.
5. Modeling, checking, and guided practice:	While viewing videotape make up a list of ten important differences between the film and the original story. (40 minutes)
6. Closure:	See guidelines for writing your own resolution to the story and for writing an essay on why Faulkner would not have approved the movie's resolution.

For the follow-up exercises, you must have deleted the last paragraph, the resolution, of Faulkner's story. Handout follows. Perceptive students will notice that without this paragraph, the story stops but does not end.

TEXT: Faulkner, W. (1995, Reissue). "Two Soldiers," in McDonald, E. (ed.): *Collected Stories of William Faulkner.* New York: Vintage Books.

PLOT-CHECK QUIZ ON *TWO SOLDIERS*

Directions: Choose the *best* answer by marking the scantron. Please do not mark on this test.

1. "Me and Pete," the first three words of the story, refers to:

   a. Billy Joe and his brother
   b. The narrator and his cousin
   c. The narrator and his brother

2. The narrator of the story is almost ___ years old.

   a. Nine b. Ten c. Fifteen d. Seventeen e. Twenty

3. Pete is almost ___ years old.

   a. Nine b. Ten c. Fifteen d. Seventeen e. Twenty

4. Most of the story takes place in:

   a. Memphis
   b. Oxford
   c. Frenchman's Bend
   d. Mississippi
   e. Jefferson

5. The time of the story is during the____World War.

   a. First b. Second c. Both of these d. Neither of these

6. Pete goes to the city to:

   a. Enlist in the Army
   b. Get a job
   c. Go to school
   d. Pay a debt
   e. None of these

7. When Pete left home, he was most concerned about the effect his absence would have on his:

   a. Maw b. Pap c. brother d. sister e. None of these

8. Pete's mother is *against* his leaving home because:

   a. She can't think of one good reason.

b. She thinks that her brother did enough in the past.
c. She knows he will get into trouble.
d. She thinks his brother will want to leave home next.
e. None of these.

9. Pete's father is *against* his leaving home because:

a. He had done enough already.
b. He needed Pete's help on the farm.
c. He had gotten into trouble himself.
d. He agreed with Pete's mother's thinking.
e. None of these.

10. Pete's brother is both *for and against* his brother's leaving home.

a. True b. False.

11. Since Pete felt that he had to leave home, that he's *"got to go,"* his brother assumed that he would have to go with him.

a. True b. False

12. Pete never did give a reason for leaving home.

a. True b. False.

13. The author wants us to admire Pete's reason for leaving home.

a. True b. False.

14. The author wants us to think that Pete's brother is foolish for wanting to leave home with his brother.

a. True b. False

15. Pete's brother finally gets to the city where Pete had gone by:

a. Walking
b. Walking and riding
c. Hitchhiking
d. Bus
e. Train

16. When Pete finally gets to Memphis and finds his brother, Pete is:

a. Bewildered
b. Astonished
c. Disgusted

d. Angry
e. Embarrassed

17. Pete immediately reprimands his brother for:
    a. Using profane language
    b. Using his knife
    c. Whining and whimpering
    d. Disobeying him
    e. Not telling his parents he had also left home
18. Peter's brother told him that he had come to Memphis because:
    a. He wanted to say good-by
    b. His heart hurt
    c. He knew he wanted him to come
    d. He knew he would need wood and water
    e. None of these
19. Pete's brother is astonished when his older brother:
    a. Hits him on the head
    b. Told him he had embarrassed him
    c. Kisses him
    d. Screams at him for coming to find him
    e. None of these
20. Pete's brother returned home because he knew:
    a. He was too young to remain
    b. His parents would be worried that he had run away
    c. His brother told him to do so
    d. He needed more money
    e. He really could not be of any help

EXERCISES ON THE RESOLUTION OF *TWO SOLDIERS*

EXERCISE 1

Write your own resolution to the story. You probably noticed that this story stops but does not end (the last paragraph has been omitted). It has no resolution.

- *Begin* by listing any question or questions about the story that seem unanswered. *Why do you still want to know about Pete's brother?*
- *Reread the last page* of the story beginning with the sentence, "She had a car." Be sure to make notations on your copy about the way the boy tells his story.
- What is distinctive or unique about the style of the story teller, Pete's little brother? Try to be as specific as possible.
- *Write your own resolution to the story.* Try to anticipate how you think Faulkner ends his story. Write a resolution to the story that answers the above question(s) *and* imitates the style and tone of the nine-year old narrator.

EXERCISE 2

Compare the five student model resolutions (handout follows) with the original. Which is closest to Faulkner's in style and tone?

How close did *you* come to Faulkner's ending? How can you explain the differences? *Explain your answer in a paragraph on your own paper.*

EXERCISE 3 (OPTIONAL/EXTRA CREDIT)

Revise in Standard (correct) English (on your own paper) the concluding paragraph of Faulkner's story. Compare your revision with the author's original paragraph. *What has happened to the tone of the passage? Why?*

EXERCISE 4

How does the movie version of the story end? Why would Faulkner have disapproved of this ending? Begin with a topic sentence that states the difference between the two endings and then *explain in a one-page essay,* two or three reasons for Faulkner's rejection of the movie's resolution.

STUDENT RESOLUTIONS OF *TWO SOLDIERS*

Discussion: Which one of these student resolutions to the short story best imitates the style and tone of the nine-year-old narrator?

(1)

We had drove fer 'bout fifteen minutes an I fell asleep. I reckon it was 'bout an hour before I was waked up. We was in some town at a eatin place an we et some mighty good ham 'n eggs 'n I had most of what seemed like a pot of coffee. The soldier paid fer the food an didn't stop-a-tall 'till we was home and he waked me up again so's I gitted outa the car an walked up to the door and went in.

Maw was settin in her rocker an Pap was still off in the field or sumpin. Maw said, "Well, we figgered you'd come home iffen you got hungry." I said, "I had to go to tell Pete goodby." Then Maw said, "So that's where you were. We figgered you'd done somethin' like that."

(2)

When I headed fer da car dis other soldier with lots of buttons hopped in fron of me and opened up the door. We was driven through all the town that I came though goin the other way. The soldier was very quiet and he was listen to the radio. But it was not what Pete and me listen to at Old Man Killegrew's. He was listen to some funny music with some lady hollerin in the background. About eighty miles later, my stomach made a loud noise and jest after that the soldier stopped at some nice place to eat. After we ate we left. The car drove up to the mailbox and I got out. When Maw saw me, she came runnin out of the house. She dropped to her knees and gave be a great big bear hug. Then she told me that if I ever did that again she'd beat the livin tar outa me.

(3)

Me and the driver sat in the car for two and a half hours and said nothing. As we was gettin into Jefferson County, I asked the soldier, "Would you watch o'er my Pete for me?" The soldier said Pete would be just fine. When we got to the mail box, I got out, said 'bye and he was gone. My legs were wobblin as I got to the door. Before I knowed it, there was Maw and Paw to get me a big ole hug. While we was all crying, Maw said, "I can't lose you too, darlin." I asked, "Don't you wanna know where I was?" "We don't care since you're home now." After supper, I had to go to sleep. Before I left the room I heard Maw and Paw say, "We love you." That next mornin at break of day, I was out workin Pete's ten acres.

THE AUTHOR'S RESOLUTION OF *TWO SOLDIERS*

Then we was gone again. And now I could see Memphis good, bright in the sunshine, while we was swinging around it. And the first thing I knowed, we was back on the same highway the bus run on this morning—the patches of stores and them big gins and sawmills, and Memphis running on for miles, it seemed like to me, before it begun to give out. Then we was running again between the fields and woods, running fast now, and except for that soldier, it was like I hadn't never been to Memphis a-tall. We was going fast now. At this rate, before I knowed it we would be home again, and I thought about me riding up to Frenchman's Bend in this big car with a soldier running it, and all of a sudden I begun to cry. I never knowed I was fixing to, and I couldn't stop it. I set there by that soldier, crying. We was going fast.

LESSON PLAN 13: *THANK YOU M'AM*

1. Focus:	Journal writing: Have you ever been caught stealing? What happened? How did you feel then? How do you feel now? If you have never been caught stealing, has one of your friends? What was your reaction? Did you try to help him or her question (10 minutes)
2. Objective:	To solve several questions of interpretation about the overall meaning of the story.
3. Purpose:	To increase our mutual understanding (comprehension) and, as a result, our enjoyment of the story. To develop the habit of independent and critical thinking.
4. Input:	Begin with a factual quiz to check that everyone has read the story. Handout follows. (Rule 1: No one may participate who has not read the selection.) The quiz should be ten factual questions, short answers (not True/False). Those with 70% are in the inner circle; those with less are in the outer circle. (15 minutes) Three basic questions. Handout follows. (30 or 60 minutes)
5. Modeling, checking, and guided practice:	During discussion the co-leaders model the four rules of discussion, and check for understanding by asking follow-up questions for clarification, substantiation, consistency, relevance, implication, resolution, and to get more opinion. Guided practice is the discussion.
6. Closure:	Oral or written resolution of one or two basic questions just discussed.

During Socratic Seminar day(s), in a full 90-minute period, four pairs of student co-leaders each lead a 15-minute discussion of the reading. It is important that the teacher approves the student co-leaders' questions before discussion to avoid wasting time on questions that are not clear, are factual, or evaluative. (Discussion should center on solving problems, not on trying to figure out what the problems are.) During the remaining time (if any) the teacher leads a demonstration discussion (modeling) of one of his or her basic questions on the reading of the lesson.

TEXT: Hughes, L. (1977). "Thank You M'am," in Redman, E. C. (ed.): *Introduction to the Short Story.* Florence, KY: McCormick-Mathers.

PLOT-CHECK QUIZ FOR *THANK YOU M'AM*

Directions: First, answer each question briefly in a complete sentence in the space beneath it. Second, label the kind of question by marking at the left *Fact* for factual, *Int* for interpretation, and *Eval* for evaluation.

_____ 1. Why does Mrs. Jones think Roger tried to steal her purse?

_____ 2. What does Mrs. Jones mean when she says, "You put yourself in contact with me"?

_____ 3. Would you try to help someone who had stolen from you?

_____ 4. Does Mrs. Jones ask about Roger's background?

_____ 5. Why isn't Mrs. Jones angry when Roger tells her why he tried to steal her purse?

_____ 6. Do you believe that most people would respond well if they were taught that stealing is wrong in a loving way?

_____ 7. What is meant by: "He [Roger] did not trust the woman not to trust him"?

_____ 8. During his stay with Mrs. Jones, could Roger have run away?

_____ 9. How does Mrs. Jones teach Roger that stealing is wrong?

_____ 10. Why does Roger want to say "something other than "thank you, M'am" when he leaves Mrs. Jones' apartment?

ANSWER KEY

Factual (1, 4, and 8); Interpretation (2, 5, 7, 9 and 10); Evaluation (3 and 6).

BASIC QUESTION FOR *THANK YOU M'AM*

Does Mrs. Jones help Roger mainly because she views him as a son?

If *no*, then:

1. Why does she tell Roger that he ought to be her son and repeatedly refer to him as "son"? (pp. 131, 133, 134)
2. Why is Mrs. Jones so concerned about Roger's physical appearance? (p. 131, 132)
3. Why does Mrs. Jones tell Roger that he could have *asked* her for the money for the shoes? (p. 132)
4. Why does the author want Mrs. Jones to know that Roger had no one at home? (pp. 131, 132)
5. Why does Mrs. Jones give Roger money to buy shoes even though he has not asked for it? (p. 134)

If *yes*, then:

6. When Mrs. Jones puts Roger out of her apartment why does she call him "boy"? (p. 134)
7. Are we to believe that Mrs. Jones would have helped *anyone* who had tried to steal from her?
8. What does Mrs. Jones mean when she tells Roger that when she gets through with him, he'll remember her? (p. 31)
9. Does Mrs. Jones want to share her supper with Roger only because she thought that he was hungry? (p. 132)
10. Why doesn't Mrs. Jones "yell at" or lecture Roger about stealing?

ALTERNATIVE BASIC QUESTIONS

Here are two more basic questions that you can qualify for discussion if you can come up with at least eight related interpretive follow-up questions for each. When students are struggling to write their own basic questions, I sometimes give them a basic question as an intermediate step to writing their own clusters. They then have to develop at least eight of their own related interpretive follow-up questions.

BASIC QUESTION NO. 2

Does the author suggest that Mrs. Jones and Roger need each other?

BASIC QUESTION NO. 3

How does Mrs. Jones teach Roger right from wrong?

CAVEAT

The model basic questions that accompany the Lesson Plan for each reading are *not* intended to be ready-made questions that you can try out on a group. The issues they raise, the questions they pose, are meant to make you think harder and better about *your own* questions. To be sure, next to asking good spontaneous follow-up questions, the hardest part of the Socratic method is coming up with your own questions about the readings. Why? There are no answer keys for discussion and because thinking is difficult! Nevertheless, the rewards are great.

LESSON PLAN 14: *CHARLES*

1. Focus:	Journal writing: Have you ever lied to your parents about an important matter? Why? How did you feel then? What happened as a result? How do you feel now? Did you ever tell them the truth? Why? What happened? (10 minutes)
2. Objective:	To solve several questions of interpretation about the overall meaning of the story.
3. Purpose:	To increase our mutual understanding (comprehension) and, as a result, our enjoyment of the story. To develop the habit of independent and critical thinking.
4. Input:	Begin with a factual quiz to check that everyone has read the story Handout follows. (Rule 1: No one may participate who has not read the selection.) The quiz should be ten factual questions, short answers (not True/False). Those with 70% are in the inner circle; those with less are in the outer circle. (15 minutes) Two basic questions. (30 or 60 minutes)
5. Modeling, checking, and guided practice:	During discussion the co-leaders model the four rules of discussion, and check for understanding by asking follow-up questions for clarification, substantiation, consistency, relevance, implication, resolution, and to get more opinion. Guided practice is the discussion.
6. Closure:	Oral or written resolution of one or two basic questions just discussed.

During Socratic Seminar day(s), in a full 90-minute period, four pairs of student co-leaders each lead a 15-minute discussion of the reading. It is important that the teacher approves the student co-leaders' questions before discussion to avoid wasting time on questions that are not clear, are factual, or evaluative. (Discussion should center on solving problems, not on trying to figure out what the problems are.) During the remaining time (if any) the teacher leads a demonstration discussion (modeling) of one of his or her basic questions on the reading of the lesson.

TEXT: Jackson, S. (1953). *Life Among the Savages* (pp. 23–30). New York: Crowell-Collier. *Charles* was originally published as a short story in *Mademoiselle*.

PLOT-CHECK QUIZ FOR *CHARLES*

Directions: First, answer each question briefly in a complete sentence in the space beneath it. Second, label the kind of question by marking at the left *Fact* for factual, *Int* for interpretation, and *Eval* for evaluation.

_____ 1. How does Laurie show that he likes talking about Charles?

_____ 2. Does Laurie treat his father the same way that he does his mother?

_____ 3. Why does Laurie invent Charles?

_____ 4. Have you ever made up a story about an imaginary friend?

_____ 5. Why did Laurie stay after school when Charles was bad?

_____ 6. Why does the kindergarten teacher refer to Laurie as "a fine little helper, with occasional lapses, of course"?

_____ 7. Were Laurie's parents too permissive?

_____ 8. Why does Laurie's mother want "passionately" to meet Charles' mother?

_____ 9. Why did the teacher have to tell Laurie's parents that there was no Charles in kindergarten?

_____ 10. Why do Laurie's parents never catch on that Laurie invented Charles?

ANSWER KEY

Factual (1, 2, 5, and 9); Interpretation (3, 6, 8, and 10); Evaluation (4 and 7).

BASIC QUESTION FOR *CHARLES*

Why does Laurie invent Charles?

1. Why does Laurie like so much to talk about Charles? (pp. 2, 4, 6)
2. Why does Laurie report "grimly" when Charles is good for a while? (p. 3)
3. Why does Laurie make Charles bigger than himself? (p. 3)
4. Why does Laurie avoid telling his parents Charles' last name? (p. 3)
5. Why does Laurie note that Charles doesn't wear rubbers or even a jacket? (p. 3)
6. Why does Laurie hesitate when he gives the name Charles to the imaginary boy in kindergarten? (p. 1)
7. Why does Laurie "demand" that his parents listen to his talk of Charles? (p. 2, 4)
8. Why does Laurie whisper joyfully the bad word that Charles said twice? (p. 3)
9. Does Laurie invent Charles because he thinks his parents are dumb? (p. 1)
10. Does Laurie invent Charles to be able to talk about himself indirectly?

ALTERNATIVE BASIC QUESTION

Here are three more basic questions that you can qualify for discussion if you can come up with at least eight related interpretive follow-up questions for each. When students are struggling to write their own basic questions, I sometimes give them a basic question as an intermediate step to writing their own clusters. They then have to develop at least eight of their own related interpretive follow-up questions.

BASIC QUESTION NO. 2

Why do his parents never realize that Laurie invented Charles until his teacher told them that there was no Charles?

CAVEAT

The model basic questions that accompany the Lesson Plan for each reading are *not* intended to be ready-made questions that you can try out on a group. The issues they raise, the questions they pose, are meant to make you think harder and better about *your own* questions. To be sure, next to asking good spontaneous follow-up questions, the hardest part of the Socratic method is coming up with your own questions about the readings. Why? There are no answer keys for discussion and because thinking is difficult! Nevertheless, the rewards are great.

LESSON PLAN 15: *SUCKER*

1. Focus:	Journal writing: Has a girl friend or a boy friend ever suddenly dumped you and you could not understand why? If so, how did you react? Did you try to remedy the situation? If so, why so? If not, why not? How do you feel about it today? (10 minutes)
2. Objective:	To solve several questions of interpretation about the overall meaning of the story.
3. Purpose:	To increase our mutual understanding (comprehension) and, as a result, our enjoyment of the story. To develop the habit of independent and critical thinking.
4. Input:	Begin with a factual quiz to check that everyone has read the story Handout follows. (Rule 1: No one may participate who has not read the selection.) The quiz should be ten factual questions, short answers (not True/False). Those with 70% are in the inner circle; those with less are in the outer circle. (15 minutes) Two basic questions. Handout follows (30 or 60 minutes)
5. Modeling, checking, and guided practice:	During discussion the co-leaders model the four rules of discussion, and check for understanding by asking follow-up questions for clarification, substantiation, consistency, relevance, implication, resolution, and to get more opinion. Guided practice is the discussion.
6. Closure:	Oral or written resolution of one or two basic questions just discussed.

During Socratic Seminar day(s), in a full 90-minute period, four pairs of student co-leaders each lead a 15-minute discussion of the reading. It is important that the teacher approves the student co-leaders' questions before discussion to avoid wasting time on questions that are not clear, are factual, or evaluative. (Discussion should center on solving problems, not on trying to figure out what the problems are.) During the remaining time (if any) the teacher leads a demonstration discussion (modeling) of one of his or her basic questions on the reading of the lesson.

TEXT: McCullers, C. (1965). "Sucker," in Abrams, W. (ed.): *Prize Stories: The O. Henry Awards*. Garden City, NY: Doubleday.

PLOT-CHECK QUIZ FOR *SUCKER*

Directions: First, answer each question briefly in a complete sentence in the space beneath it. Second, label the kind of question by marking at the left *Fact* for factual, *Int* for interpretation, and *Eval* for evaluation.

_____ 1. Why does Pete give the nickname Sucker to his cousin?

_____ 2. Why does Pete look back on his damaged relationship with Sucker?

_____ 3. Why does Sucker wait so long to get out on his own and hang around with the other kids?

_____ 4. Does Pete think that Sucker was dumb for doing whatever he told him to do?

_____ 5. Have you ever been unable to apologize to someone you had hurt?

_____ 6. How was Pete mean to Sucker?

_____ 7. Why does the author make Sucker younger than Pete but Maybelle older than Pete?

_____ 8. Why is Pete mean to Sucker when Maybelle begins to ignore him?

_____ 9. Do you dream about things that worry or bother you?

_____ 10. Does Pete admit that he liked Sucker more than anybody else—even Maybelle?

ANSWER KEY

Factual (2, 4, and 6); Interpretation (1, 3, 7, and 8); Evaluation (5 and 9)

BASIC QUESTION ON *SUCKER*

Does Pete look back on his relationship with Sucker to find a way to make up with him or to excuse his own mean actions towards Sucker?

1. Why does Pete qualify so many statements with "I guess" or "I suppose" or "maybe I would have acted differently"? (pp. 20, 21, 26, 28, 30)
2. Does Pete use his painful experience with Maybelle to excuse his own meanness towards Sucker? (pp. 20, 21, 23, 27, 28)
3. Is Pete excusing himself when he says what happened at night made things how they are now between himself and Sucker? (pp. 22, 27)
4. Why does Pete says he couldn't help himself when he told off Sucker? (p. 27)
5. Are we to believe it *is* Sucker's fault that Pete cannot apologize to him? (p. 29)
6. Why does Pete admit he feels guilty that people tend to despise those who admire them a lot? (p. 20)
7. Is Pete sincere when he says he did like Sucker "more than anybody else [he] knew"? (p. 23)
8. Why does Pete realize that he hurt Sucker so much more deeply because his voice was slow and calm when he told him off? (p. 28)
9. Why does it bother Pete so much that he can do nothing to get his relationship with Sucker restored? (p. 30)
10. Why is Pete still uneasy in his mind three months after his break-up with Sucker? (p. 29)

ALTERNATIVE BASIC QUESTION

Here is another basic question that you can qualify for discussion if you can come up with at least eight related interpretive follow-up questions for each. When students are struggling to write their own basic questions, I sometimes give them a basic question as an intermediate step to writing their own clusters. They then have to develop at least eight of their own related interpretive follow-up questions.

BASIC QUESTION NO. 2

Why does Pete's relationship with Sucker depend on his relationship with Maybelle?

CAVEAT

The model basic questions that accompany the Lesson Plan for each reading are *not* intended to be ready-made questions that you can try out on a group. The issues they raise, the questions they pose, are meant to make you think harder and better about *your own* questions. To be sure, next to asking good spontaneous follow-up questions, the hardest part of the Socratic method is coming up with your own questions about the readings. Why? There are no answer keys for discussion and because thinking is difficult! Nevertheless, the rewards are great.

LESSON PLAN 16: *THERE WILL COME SOFT RAINS*

1. Focus:	Is it possible to write a short story in which there are no live characters? (Ray Bradbury has done it!)
2. Objective:	To solve several questions of interpretation about the overall meaning of the story.
3. Purpose:	To increase our mutual understanding (comprehension) and, as a result, our enjoyment of the story. To develop the habit of independent and critical thinking.
4. Input:	Begin with a factual quiz to check that everyone has read the story Handouts follow. (Rule 1: No one may participate who has not read the selection.) The quiz should be ten factual questions, short answers (not true/false). Those with 70% are in the inner circle; those with less are in the outer circle. (15 minutes) Two basic questions. (30 or 60 minutes)
5. Modeling, checking, and guided practice:	During discussion the co-leaders model the four rules of discussion, and check for understanding by asking follow-up questions for clarification, substantiation, consistency, relevance, implication, resolution, and to get more opinion. Guided practice is the discussion.
6. Closure:	Oral or written resolution of one or two basic questions just discussed.

During Socratic Seminar day(s), in a full 90-minute period, four pairs of student co-leaders each lead a 15-minute discussion of the reading. It is important that the teacher approves the student co-leaders' questions before discussion to avoid wasting time on questions that are not clear, are factual, or evaluative. (Discussion should center on solving problems, not on trying to figure out what the problems are.) During the remaining time (if any) the teacher leads a demonstration discussion (modeling) of one of his or her basic questions on the reading of the lesson.

TEXT: Bradbury, R. (1965). "There Will Come Soft Rains," in *The Vintage Bradbury* (pp. 322–329). New York: Vintage Books.

PLOT-CHECK QUIZ ON *THERE WILL COME SOFT RAINS*

Directions: First, answer each question in the space beneath it in a complete sentence. Second, at the left of each question's number, identify the kind of question by marking *Fact* for factual, *Int* for interpretation, and *Eval* for evaluation.

_____ 1. How does Bradbury compare the death of the house to a human death?

_____ 2. Why does Bradbury want us to somehow feel sad about the death of the house?

_____ 3. Why did Bradbury make the first line of Sara Teasdale's poem the story's title?

_____ 4. Why does the poem suggest that nature would be indifferent to man's survival?

_____ 5. How did the house provide for the needs of the McCullan family?

_____ 6. Why does Bradbury emphasize all the services the house provided for this family?

_____ 7. Why does Bradbury describe the actions of the house as "the ritual of a religion"?

_____ 8. Would you like to live in a house like the McCullan's? If so, why so? If not, why not?

_____ 9. Why does Bradbury have the house survive a nuclear blast but succumb to fire?

_____ 10. How much time does the story cover?

ANSWER KEY FOR PLOT-CHECK QUIZ ON *THERE WILL COME SOFT RAINS*

Directions: First, answer each question in the space beneath it in a complete sentence. Second, at the left of each question's number, identify the kind of question by marking *Fact* for factual, *Int* for interpretation, and *Eval* for evaluation.

1. How does Bradbury compare the *death* of the house to a human death?

   Fact: In several ways—over a dozen. For example, he refers to the attic brain.

2. Why does Bradbury want us to somehow feel sad about the death of the house?

   Int: *Yes* can be as correct as *no* depending on the supporting textual evidence.

3. Why did Bradbury make the first line of Sara Teasdale's poem the story's title?

   Int: More than one correct answer is possible. For example, he may want to refer to the poem's theme that nature is indifferent to what mankind does.

4. Why does the poem suggest that nature would be indifferent to man's survival?

   Int: More than one correct answer is possible.

5. How did the house provide for the needs of the McCullan family?

   Fact: In many ways. It fed them, warmed their beds, etc.

6. Why does Bradbury emphasize all the services the house provided for this family?

   Int: More than one answer is possible.

7. Why does Bradbury describe the actions of the house as "the ritual of a religion"?

   Int: More than one answer is possible.

8. Would you like to live in a house like the McCullan's? If so, why so? If not, why not?

   Eval: A question about personal values.

9. Why does Bradbury have the house survive a nuclear blast but succumb to fire?

   Int: More than one answer is possible.

10. How much time does the story cover?

    Fact: One complete day in the *life* of the McCullan house.

BASIC QUESTIONS FOR *THERE WILL COME SOFT RAINS*

Here are two basic questions that you can qualify for discussion if you can come up with at least eight related interpretive follow-up questions for each. When students are struggling to write their own basic questions, I sometimes give them a basic question as an intermediate step to writing their own clusters. They then have to develop at least eight of their own related interpretive follow-up questions.

BASIC QUESTION NO. 1

Why does Bradbury compare the death of the house to the death of a human being?

BASIC QUESTION NO. 2

Why does Bradbury use the first line of Sara Teasdale's poem as the title for his story? (The text of Teasdale's poem appears below.)

CAVEAT

The model basic questions that accompany the Lesson Plan for each reading are *not* intended to be ready-made questions that you can try out on a group. The issues they raise, the questions they pose, are meant to make you think harder and better about *your own* questions. To be sure, next to asking good spontaneous follow-up questions, the hardest part of the Socratic method is coming up with your own questions about the readings. Why? There are no answer keys for discussion and because thinking is difficult! Nevertheless, the rewards are great.

LESSON PLAN 17: *THE ZODIACS*

1. Focus:	Journal Writing: Have you ever played on a team that had been a loser but became a winner? Or: Has your playing intermural sports been a good or bad experience. Explain. (10 minutes)
2. Objective:	To solve several questions of interpretation about the overall meaning of the story.
3. Purpose:	To increase our mutual understanding (comprehension) and, as a result, our enjoyment of the story. To develop the habit of independent and critical thinking.
4. Input:	Begin with a factual quiz to check that everyone has read the story Handout follows. (Rule 1: No one may participate who has not read the selection.) The quiz should be ten factual questions, short answers (not True/False). Those with 70% are in the inner circle; those with less are in the outer circle. (15 minutes) Three basic questions. Handout follows (30 or 60 minutes)
5. Modeling, checking, and guided practice:	During discussion the co-leaders model the four rules of discussion, and check for understanding by asking follow-up questions for clarification, substantiation, consistency, relevance, implication, resolution, and to get more opinion. Guided practice is the discussion.
6. Closure:	Oral or written resolution of one or two basic questions just discussed.

During Socratic Seminar day(s), in a full 90-minute period, four pairs of student co-leaders each lead a 15-minute discussion of the reading. It is important that the teacher approves the student co-leaders' questions before discussion to avoid wasting time on questions that are not clear, are factual, or evaluative. (Discussion should center on solving problems, not on trying to figure out what the problems are.) During the remaining time (if any) the teacher leads a demonstration discussion (modeling) of one of his or her basic questions on the reading of the lesson.

TEXT: Neugeboren, J. (1992). *The Zodiacs.* Chicago: Great Books Foundation.

PLOT-CHECK QUIZ FOR *THE ZODIACS*

Directions: Answer each question in a complete sentence in the space beneath it.

1. Why does Louie want to manage the team?

2. Why does the author make Louie the worst athlete in the school but the smartest kid in his class?

3. How did Louie get George to agree to play for the Zodiacs?

4. Did both Louie and George contribute to the success of the Zodiacs?

5. Have you ever played on a team that had been a loser but became a winner?

6. What is George's opinion of his brother?

7. Why does the narrator of the story admire Louie so much?

8. Why does Louie try to get George back on the team?

9. If you were Louie, what would you have done when George hit you?

10. What did Louie do after George hit him?

BASIC QUESTION FOR *THE ZODIACS*

Why does the author make both George and Louie responsible for the success of the Zodiacs?

1. Why does the author make George older and a gang member unlike the other boys on the team? (p. 47)
2. Why is George made not only a good pitcher but also a good hitter? (p. 51)
3. Why does the author give George a brother who has been in jail? (p. 47)
4. Why does the author make Louie the worst athlete in school but also the smartest kid in his class? (p. 44)
5. Why does Louie want to manage a losing team? (pp. 44–46)
6. Why does the author have Louie excel in getting "a good press" as well as in organizing the team?
7. Why does Jimmy O'Brien's column mention bother George and Louie's victrola? (p. 51)
8. Why does the author have the Zodiac's first game delayed until George and Louie arrive? (pp. 49–50)

ALTERNATIVE BASIC QUESTIONS

Here are two more basic questions that you can qualify for discussion if you can come up with at least eight related interpretive follow-up questions for each. When students are struggling to write their own basic questions, I sometimes give them a basic question as an intermediate step to writing their own clusters. They then have to develop at least eight of their own related interpretive follow-up questions.

BASIC QUESTION NO. 2

Why does the narrator admire Louie so much?

BASIC QUESTION NO. 3

Why does the author have George and Louis clash over the raffle money?

CAVEAT

The model basic questions that accompany the Lesson Plan for each reading are *not* intended to be ready-made questions that you can try out on a group. The issues they raise, the questions they pose, are meant to make you think harder and better about *your own* questions. To be sure, next to asking good spontaneous follow-up questions, the hardest part of the Socratic method is coming up with your own questions about the readings. Why? There are no answer keys for discussion and because thinking is difficult! Nevertheless, the rewards are great.

LESSON PLAN 18: *BETHGELERT*

1. Focus:	Journal writing: "Literature was not born on the day when a boy crying 'wolf, wolf' came running out of the Neanderthal valley with a big gray wolf at his heels. Literature was born on the day when a boy came crying 'wolf, wolf' and there was no wolf." (Vladimir Nabokov) Why did literature begin when there was no wolf? (10 minutes:)
2. Objective:	To review the six elements of the short story: plot, character, theme, tone, setting, and point of view.
3. Purpose:	To understand why tone is the most important element—that all other elements establish the tone of the story. To misunderstand tone is to miss the meaning.
4. Input:	List student answers to the question about why literature began when there was no wolf.
5. Modeling:	Review the definitions of the six elements of the short story. Ask for an example of each element in *Bethgelert*.
6. Checking, and guided practice:	First reading and notations on *Bethgelert*. Handout follows. Review notations. Ask for an example of each element of the short story in *Bethgelert*.
7. Closure:	Conclude with a discussion of the story. What does the last line of the story mean (theme): "I repent me as much as the man who slew his greyhound."?

This lesson is a good follow up to Lesson 19 on the good or value of reading and studying literature.

TEXT: Spencer, W. (1998). "Bethgelert," in *Celtic Fairy Tales.* Bristol, England: Paragon.

LESSON PLAN 19: *THE ZEBRA STORYTELLER*

1. Focus:	Journal topic: What is the good or value of reading and even studying literature (fiction)? (10 minutes)
2. Objective:	To compare and contrast several answers to the basic question about the good or value of studying imaginative literature.
3. Purpose:	To reflect on several answers to this most basic question at the beginning of our study of English.
4. Input:	List student answers to the journal question on the overhead. Then have them read the article by Moeller and "The Zebra Storyteller." Ask them to choose the single most important reason for studying literature that they found in the reading.
5. Modeling:	Review Moeller's answers to the basic question about the value of literatue.
6. Checking, and guided practice:	Ask for an example of some story that illustrates each of the reasons for studying literature in the article. An alternative follow-up activity is to read and discuss *Bethgelert,* the one-page story by Spencer, in Lesson Plan 18.
7. Closure:	Review what they now regard as the most important reason for reading and studying literature.

TEXT: Holst, S. (1993). "The Zebra Storyteller," in *The Zebra Storyteller: Collected Stories.* Barrytown, NY: Station Hill Press.

WHY DO WE READ AND EVEN STUDY LITERATURE? BY VICTOR J. MOELLER

1. The most obvious reason has to be that stories are entertaining and amusing. With imaginative literature, there is something to satisfy everyone's taste—from romance, to gothic tales, to mystery, to westerns, to science-fiction, to whatever! Look around. Be a browser. Talk to a reader.
2. Reading stories also *educates our imaginations*. Those who think that a story like "The Zebra Storyteller" is dumb or stupid, have not developed their imaginations. In fiction, anything can happen and an author does not have to prove anything. Our only obligation as readers is to understand the world that an author has placed us in—not to argue about the author's creation. If we do so, we can increase our enjoyment immensely. Unless we develop our imaginations, we will remain literal-minded and foolishly demand that all stories be true-to-life. How dull that would be.
3. On the other hand, the contrast between the real or actual and the extraordinary or the fanciful, suggests two different uses that readers make of imaginative literature. Sometimes we *do* want to read about people like ourselves, or about places, things, experiences, and ideas that we are familiar with and make us feel comfortable. In the process of reading about situations related to our own lives, *we can learn more about ourselves and the world about us.* Realism will always have its appeal.
4. But at other times, the last thing that we want is a story about people like ourselves or experiences similar to those in our everyday lives. We might be accused of wanting *to escape.* We want something *different or strange*—like Stephen King stories. We want to get out of ourselves and the confining, all-too-familiar, and learn that there are other ways of looking at the world besides our own. In short, we want to read about exotic places, about other worlds that have never existed, or worlds that may never exist. The romantic spirit will always contend with realism's appeal.
5. Stories also prepare us for the unexpected and help us *to avoid projecting false hopes and fears* (such as superstitious zebras who think that they are being preyed on by the ghosts of lions) and show us what we can actually expect in our everyday lives. Because some people never train their imagination to project any other "story" than their

own, they cannot conceive of any other shape for their expectations. As a result, they remain stunted and naive about life.

6. Finally, reading stories can put us in closer touch with our feelings. Good stories, powerful stories, revulse us at what is ugly and cruel and mean in life. On the other hand, stories can also inspire us to marvel at what is good and wonderful and beautiful in life. Recall George's devotion to Lennie or Nick Carraway's refusal to become as self-serving as those about him. In short, some stories can be so terrible that they may move us to tears and prompt us to say, "That's the way life must never be," while others are so poignant that we find ourselves saying, "That's the way life ought to be," or, "That's the way life could be!"

LESSON PLAN 20: *GASTON*

1. Focus:	Journal topic: How does a parent's divorce affect their children? (10 minutes)
2. Objective:	To solve several questions of interpretation about the overall meaning of the story.
3. Purpose:	To increase our mutual understanding (comprehension) and, as a result, our enjoyment of the story.
4. Input:	Begin with a factual quiz to check that everyone has read the novel Handout follows. (Rule 1: No one may participate who has not read the selection.) The quiz should be ten factual questions, short answers (not True/False). Those with 70% are in the inner circle; those with less are in the outer circle. (15 minutes)
	Two or four basic questions. Handout follows (30 or 60 minutes)
5. Modeling, checking, and guided practice:	During discussion the co-leaders model the four rules of discussion, and check for understanding by asking follow-up questions for clarification, substantiation, consistency, relevance, implication, resolution, and to get more opinion. Guided practice is the discussion.
6. Closure:	Oral or written resolution of one or two basic questions just discussed.

A good follow-up lesson to this story is a discussion of Kahlil Gibran's poem "On Children," which can be found on page 16 in *The Prophet*, published in 1966 by Knopf, or on the Internet at http://www.tcp.ca/Joshuea/Children.html.

During Socratic Seminar day(s), in a full 90-minute period, four pairs of student co-leaders each lead a 15-minute discussion of the reading. It is important that the teacher approves the student co-leaders' questions before discussion to avoid wasting time on questions that are not clear, are factual, or evaluative. (Discussion should center on solving problems, not on trying to figure out what the problems are.) During the remaining time (if any) the teacher leads a demonstration discussion (modeling) of one of his or her basic questions on the reading of the lesson.

TEXT: See Figure 2.5, pages 18–23.

PLOT-CHECK QUIZ FOR *GASTON*

Directions: Put your answers on your own answer sheet; do not mark on the quiz. The answers below may be used once, more than once, or not at all.

father	mother	apples	hug
girl	New York	pears	strangers
thirty-six	forty-six	bug	close friends
Gaston	six	handsome	squashed
Braxton	ten	ugly	kiss
Paris	thirteen	funny	touch
Rome	peaches	crazy	Saint Louis

When the story opens, they (1) and (2) were to eat (3), as planned, after her nap. She (4) lived in (5) with (6) but was visiting (7) who lived in (8). "He was very old, (9) especially for a young man—he had told her; and she was (10), just up from sleep on a very hot afternoon in August." As they were eating their snack, a creature came out of a flawed (11). "*who* is it?" the girl asked. He (12) replied that it was (13). At first she was repelled by this creature but eventually came to see it as (14). When the girl wanted her own (15) with "somebody" inside it, he went to (16) to (17). While he was away, the girl received a phone call from (18) who asked if he was (19) or (20) and then told her that the creature was only a (21) that would have to be (22). The story ends abruptly when he (23) returns and discovers that she had (24).

When he asked her why she had so acted, she replied (25). As she was leaving, he was about to (26) her but decided that (27). "They shook hands like (28)." After he watched her drive off in (29), he then went around the corner where he had coffee every morning, "feeling a little, he thought, like (30) on the white plate."

ANSWER KEY FOR PLOT-CHECK QUIZ ON *GASTON*

1. The man, stranger, father
2. Little girl
3. Peaches
4. Little girl
5. New York
6. Her mother
7. Her father
8. Paris
9. Thirty-six
10. Six
11. Peach
12. Father
13. Gaston
14. Handsome
15. Peach
16. The store
17. Buy more peaches
18. Her mother
19. Crazy
20. Funny
21. Bug
22. Squashed
23. Father
24. Killed Gaston
25. "Everybody squashes bugs."
26. Hug
27. He had better not do so
28. Strangers
29. A huge limousine
30. Gaston

BASIC QUESTION FOR *GASTON*

Does Saroyan want us to conclude that the daughter or the father has more in common with Gaston's situation?

If the daughter has more in common with Gaston, then:

1. Why does the father describe Gaston as "the grand *boulevardier*"? (p. 34)
2. Does he fail to explain what a grand boulevardier is because he thinks the term applies only to himself? (pp. 34, 37)
3. Unlike the girl who wants to squash Gaston because it is ugly, why does the father think he is handsome? (p. 34)
4. Is the father telling his daughter indirectly that she, like Gaston, is "out in the world and on [her] own now"? (p. 35)
5. Why does the father say that Gaston could only *try* to live in their house? (p. 35)
6. Why does the father think it unfair for people to holler when someone comes out of his house? (p. 34)
7. Why does the girl describe Gaston's house as "broken"? (p. 37)

If the father has more in common with Gaston, then:

8. Why does the girl ask *who* the bug is rather than *what* it is? (p. 33)
9. Why does the author imply that the girl is as confused as Gaston? (p. 36)
10. Why does the girl begin to adopt her father's view of Gaston? (pp. 35–38)
11. Why does the girl cry just before she kills Gaston? (p. 38)
12. Why does the girl say that her father's house is like Gaston's? (p. 38)
13. Near the end of the story, why does Saroyan refer to the father as *the man*? (p. 38)
14. Why does the story end with the father feeling only "a little" like the squashed Gaston? (p. 39)

ALTERNATIVE BASIC QUESTION

Here is another basic question that you can qualify for discussion if you can come up with at least eight related interpretive follow-up questions for each. When students are struggling to write their own basic questions, I sometimes give them a basic question as an intermediate step to writing their own clusters. They then have to develop at least eight of their own related interpretive follow-up questions.

BASIC QUESTION NO. 2

Unlike the mother, why does the father give a name and personality to the peach worm?

CAVEAT

The model basic questions that accompany the Lesson Plan for each reading are *not* intended to be ready-made questions that you can try out on a group. The issues they raise, the questions they pose, are meant to make you think harder and better about *your own* questions. To be sure, next to asking good spontaneous follow-up questions, the hardest part of the Socratic method is coming up with your own questions about the readings. Why? There are no answer keys for discussion and because thinking is difficult! Nevertheless, the rewards are great.

DISCUSSION EXERCISE

1. The parent in *Gaston* who would have understood and agreed with the theme of *On Children* is:

   A. The mother
   B. The father
   C. Neither of them
   D. Both of them

2. In *Gaston*, the father knows that his daughter does not "belong" to him because he tells her:

   A. To go back to her mother if she wants to do so
   B. The important thing is what she wants, not what he wants
   C. That he wants her to be where she wants to be
   D. All of these

3. The mother in Saroyan's story believes that her daughter "belongs" to her because she:

   A. Gave her life
   B. Goes out of her way to influence her thinking in several ways
   C. Tries to make her feel guilty for being with her father two days
   D. Reminds her that she will have fun at the party in New York

4. The father does not seek to make his daughter "like" himself because in *Gaston* he:

   A. Does not want her to live with him unless she wants to do so
   B. Does not scold her for killing Gaston
   C. Decides not to hug her when she leaves to return to her mother
   D. All of the above

5. In Saroyan's *Gaston*, the mother tries to give her "thoughts" to her daughter when she:

   A. Asks her daughter if her father is "funny" and "crazy"
   B. Tells her daughter to squash the bug
   C. Tells her that "these two days have been like two years to me"
   D. All of the above

BIBLIOGRAPHY

RECOMMENDED FOLLOW-UP READINGS

Adler, M. J. (1967). *How to read a [great] book.* New York: Touchstone.

Adler expects you to read a book about how to read a book. What do you do? Learn how to read a book three times—at once!

Dewey, J. (1931, 1997) *How we think.* Mineola, NY: Dover.

This little classic defines the elements of reflective thinking as "(a) a state of perplexity, hesitation, doubt; and (b) a search or investigation directed toward bringing to light further facts which serve to corroborate or to nullify the suggested solution." (p. 9)

Frey, N. (1970) *The educated imagination.* Bloomington, IN: Bloomington University Press.

This series of six half-hour radio talks on the Canadian Broadcasting Corporation uses a deliberately colloquial tone to answer the most basic question about the good or value of reading and studying imaginative literature. Nothing can be more basic for an English teacher today.

Hulfinch, G., & Smith, P. (1968). *Reflective thinking: The method of education.* New York: Dodd, Mead & Co.

These two authors emphasize the two elements of Dewey's definition of reflective thinking by stating bluntly: "Where there is no problem, where no snarl appears in the normal flow of experience, there is no occasion to engage in thought....Teachers must understand the intimate relationship between problem and thought." In short, teachers waste their breath by pleading with students to think. Thinking does not begin in a vacuum; it begins only with a real problem that demands a solution.

Rosenblatt, L. (1968). *Literature as exploration.* New York: Noble and Noble.

For any English teacher this book is the companion piece to Northrup Frey's *Educated Imagination* because it explains and illustrates the teaching implications of viewing reading as a transaction between reader and text. Unless the teacher takes both into account, students will not likely become life-long readers (learners).

Sykes, C. (1995). *Dumbing down our kids: Why American children feel good about themselves but can't read, write, or add.* New York: St. Martin's Press.

By taking a historical overview of the fads and nonsense of the last seventy years of public education, Sykes argues that the school wars of the 1990s will be the defining cultural and political debate of our time. While some parents today bask in the glow of complacency about their own children's education, Sykes documents the collapse of standards in too many of our schools, the flight from serious learning, and the triumph of mediocre, feel-good education that is more concerned with developing a phony sense of self-esteem than it is with *the difficult task of developing daily the habit of independent and critical thinking.*

REFERENCES

Active Learning Practices for Schools. *The thinking classroom* http://learnweb.harvard.edu/alps/thinking/index.cfm

Adler, M. J. (1948). *A guide for leaders of great books discussion groups.* Chicago: Great Books Foundation.

Adler, M. J. (1991). *Introducing the Socratic seminar into the elementary school classroom.* Chicago: Chicago Public Schools.

Adler, M. J. (1982). *The Paideia proposal: An educational manifesto.* New York: Macmillan.

Adler, M. J. (1984). *The Paideia program.* New York: Macmillan.

Adler, M. J. (1977). *Reforming education: The opening of the American mind.* New York: Macmillan.

Adler, M. J. (1940, July 6). How to mark a book. *The Saturday Review.*

Adler, M. J. (1940). *How to read a book: The art of getting a liberal education.* New York: Simon & Schuster.

Atwell, N. (1998). *In the middle: New understanding about writing, reading, and learning.* Portsmouth, NH: Boynton/Cook.

Barthes, R. (1983). *A Barthes reader.* Sontag, S. (Ed.). New York: Noonday Press.

Bloom, B. (Ed.). (1956). *Taxonomy of educational objectives: Cognitive Domain.* New York: McKay.

Brunner, J. (1960). *The process of education.* New York: Alfred A. Knopf.

Burtness, J., Ober, K., & Seat, R. (1962). *The close reading of factual prose.* New York: Row and Peterson.

Canady, R., & Rettig, M. (1999). *Teaching in the block: Strategies for engaging active learners.* Larchmont, NY: Eye on Education.

Christenbury, L., & Kelly, P. (1983). *Questioning: A path to critical thinking.* Urbana, IL: National Council of Teachers of English.

Daniels, H. (1994). *Literature circles: Voice and choice in the student-centered classroom.* York, ME: Stenhouse Publishers.

Davis, J. (1957). *A Study of participants in the great books program.* Chicago: National Opinion Research Center, University of Chicago.

Frye, N. (1970). *The educated imagination.* Bloomington, IN: Indiana University Press.

Golub, J. (Ed.). (1986). *Activities to promote critical thinking: Classroom practices in teaching English.* Urbana, IL: National Council of Teachers of English.

Hill, R. (1957). *A comparative study of lecture and discussion methods.* Chicago: National Opinion Research Center, University of Chicago.

Holt, J. (1982). *How children fail.* Reading, PA: Perseus Books.

Holt, J. (1984). *How children learn.* Reading, PA: Perseus Books.

Hutchins, R. M. (1952). The great conversation. *Great books of the western world.* Vol. 1. Chicago: Encyclopedia Britannica.

Kaplan, A. (1957). *Study-discussion in the liberal arts.* Chicago: National Opinion Research Center, University of Chicago.

Kubler-Ross, E. (1970). *On death and dying.* New York: Macmillan.

Kutz, E., & Roskelly, H. (1991). *An unquiet pedagogy: Transforming practice in the English classroom.* Portsmouth, NH: Boynton/Cook.

Mann, T. (1969). *Magic mountain.* New York: Alfred A. Knopf, Vintage Books Edition.

Mitchell, R. (1979). *Less words can say.* Boston: Little, Brown and Company.

Moldof, E. (1965, August-September). "John Erskine: Originator and pioneer of the great books discussion program." *The Gadfly.* Chicago: Great Books Foundation.

Morris, E. (1998). *The book lover's guide to the internet.* New York: Fawcett Columbine.

National Council for Excellence in Critical Thinking. "Why teach socratically?" http://www.criticalthinking.org/ncect.ncik

Neilson, A. R. (1989). Critical thinking and reading. Urbana, IL: National Council of Teachers of English.

Provenzo, E. (1998). *The educator's brief guide to the World Wide Web.* Larchmont, NY: Eye on Education.

Reddick, R., & King, B. (1996). *The online student: Making the grade on the internet.* New York: Harcourt Brace.

Richards, I. A. (1942). *How to read [reap] a page: A course in efficient reading.* Boston: Beacon Press.

Roberts, T., & Billings, L. (1999). *The Paideia classroom: Teaching for understanding.* Larchmont, NY: Eye on Education.

Romano, T. *Clearing the way: Working with teenage writers.* Dallas, TX: Heinemann.

Rosenblatt, L. (1976). *Literature as exploration.* New York: Noble and Noble, Publishers, Inc.

Rosenblatt, L. (1978) *The reader, the text, and the poem.* Carbondale, IL: Southern Illinois University Press.

Rouse, W. H. (Trans.). (1956). *The great dialogues of Plato.* New York: Mentor.

Sanders, N. (1966). *Classroom questions: What kinds?* New York: Harper and Row.

Silberman, M. (1996). *Active learning: 101 strategies to teach any subject.* Boston: Allyn and Bacon.

Smagorinsky, P., & Whiting, M. (1995). *How English teachers get taught: Methods of teaching the methods class.* Urbana, IL: National Council of Teachers of English.

Warren, R., & Wellek, W. (1956). *Theory of literature.* New York: Harcourt, Brace.

Whitehead, A. N. (1929). *The aims of education.* New York: Macmillan.